THE HAND OF THE OJIBWA MAIDEN

A LOVE STORY SET DURING THE SIOUX REBELLION OF 1862

William Tirre

New Harbor Press
RAPID CITY, SD

Tirre/New Harbor Press
1601 Mt. Rushmore Rd., Ste 3288
Rapid City, SD 57701
www.NewHarborPress.com

Ordering Information:
Quantity sales. Special discounts are available on quantity purchases by corporations, associations, and others. For details, contact the "Special Sales Department" at the address above.

The Hand of the Ojibwa Maiden / William Tirre. -- 1st ed.
ISBN 978-1-63357-269-0

Contents

PROLOGUE

Indian-White Settler Conflicts

When two radically different cultures first encounter each other, and there is competition for some resource like arable land or forests with wild game, and neither culture has a tradition of resolving conflicts peacefully, there is likely to be violent conflict. This has been true since the first encounter between Europeans and North American Indians. From 1539 to 1543 in his quest for gold, Conquistador Hernando DeSoto and his Spanish soldiers attacked a variety of Indian tribes including the Mobile, Choctaw, Alabama, and Chickasaw in what would become the southeastern United States. In this situation, there was little or no chance of the two groups coming to some peaceful coexistence because DeSoto was in North America to conquer native nations and acquire their wealth.

Conflicts in this early period also happened even when initial contacts had been friendly. Once the Indian tribes began to feel that European settlers were encroaching on their traditional territory, conflicts would arise. Early examples of this occurred in coastal areas such as Virginia (1585-1590) resulting in the Lost Colony, and in coastal New England, (1636-1637) resulting in the Pequot War. Note that in some cases the Europeans were the aggressors and in others the Indians.

But even before Europeans arrived in North America, conflicts between Indian tribes and nations were the rule, not the exception. The concept of a "noble savage," that primitive tribal

1

people are uncorrupted by civilization and are naturally good has no basis in reality. Warfare between Indian tribes was a constant threat. Indian tribes were frequently displaced by more powerful tribes and essentially pushed into new territory. This was the origin of the long-lasting Ojibwa (Chippewa)-Santee (Sioux) feud -- the Ojibwa had pushed the Santee into the southwest corner of Minnesota. [1]

It is not known what exactly prompted the tensions between the Santee Sioux Indians and the white settlers in the northwestern corner of Iowa. But some historians trace the tensions back to an incident in 1854 instigated by a whiskey trader and horse thief named Henry Lott. Henry Lott and his son killed several Sioux including Chief Inkpaduta's blood brother Sintomniduta and his wife and their five children. We don't know why. Inkpaduta requested that the U.S. Army arrest the Lotts and bring them to justice, but Henry Lott fled and was never found. We do not know how hard the authorities searched for him; but it is possible that the search was half-hearted since much of the white population was antagonistic to the Sioux, even government officials. This was evident in the actions of Granville Berkley, the prosecuting attorney, who displayed Sintomniduta's head stuck on a pike in front of his house to express his utter contempt for the Sioux.

With these injustices and insults fresh in their memory, Sioux led by Chief Inkpaduta attacked white settlers in the Spirit Lake region. Spirit Lake was allegedly a sacred place for the Sioux, and it incensed them to see white settlers' houses on the edge of the lake. The details of this episode, which occurred in the winter of 1857, are too horrific to describe here; but by the end of their rampage, forty men, women, and children (including infants) had been killed.

In 1862 Inkpaduta took part in the Sioux Uprising in south-western Minnesota. This was a very dark period in the history of the western frontier. Chief Little Crow warned the other band chiefs that war against the white settlers was likely to be futile and fatal to the Sioux, but he was regarded as the best chief to lead the Sioux in war. Between six to eight hundred white settlers were killed in New Ulm and its vicinity, and three hundred were captured. Eventually, the uprising was put down by U.S. soldiers from Fort Snelling. In the end, thirty-eight Sioux were arrested and hanged in Mankato, Minnesota. But Inkapaduta escaped, only to reappear in 1876 at the Battle of the Little Bighorn. He survived this battle and migrated to Manitoba, taking refuge in Sitting Bull's band, and dying in 1881.

CHAPTER ONE

Minnesota River August 1859

Robert, a boy about 15 years of age, set off from his family's farm near the New Ulm settlement after finishing his morning chores. Carrying a fishing pole and a bucket of bait, the boy was hoping to find a good fishing spot on the Minnesota River, preferably shaded because the sun was already bearing down on his thick dark blonde hair. The boy was handsome with blue eyes and a complexion tanned from many hours in the sun. At first glance, this boy appeared to be just another American settler of European descent in New Ulm, Minnesota. But a closer examination suggested a mixed heritage. French Canadians would call him a métis because he was the offspring of Henri Perrault, a French American fur trader turned farmer, and his Santee Sioux wife Makawee (Sioux for freely giving and motherly).

Robert spent most of his free time alone. He did not have friends among the white boys in the vicinity and it wasn't because he was unpleasant or unfriendly. No, it was because he had "Indian blood" that the other boys shunned him. It especially did not help his situation that there was rising tension between the white farmers and the Santee Sioux Indians in Minnesota and adjoining areas in the Iowa and Dakota territories. Although he would not admit it to himself, Robert needed friendship as much as anyone else, and his loneliness was like an ever-constant dull ache.

As he picked his way around a cluster of thick bushes on the riverbank, he suddenly felt a swoosh of air pass by his face. He shouted in surprise and then turned to see an Indian boy about his age with his bow raised. The Indian boy was just as surprised as Robert. Then the two boys began shouting at each other.

"Fool, I could have killed you -- I thought you were a deer!"

"You shoot deer when they come to the river for a drink?"

"Yes, you must catch them off guard. And when there is a good harvest of corn, I set out corn for them to eat and I shoot them from my deer blind."

"Doesn't seem very sporting to me, killing an animal while it drinks or eats."

The Santee Sioux don't hunt for sport; they hunt to eat! Remember that. So, what do you have in your bucket?"

"I've got some minnows and earthworms as fish bait. I'm looking for a shady spot on the river where the fishing is good."

"Ha! Just as I thought! Then when they bite the bait for a quick meal you hook them, and you pull them in. How is that different from what I was doing?" The shouting subsided as the boys calmed down.

"Well, I get your point. We are both killing a living animal to eat. Here, let's start over right. My name is Robert."

"In your language, my name is Snowy Owl. In Santee Sioux, it is*hiŋháŋ ská.*"

"That's a coincidence! My mother used to call me that when I was a little child because my hair was snowy white."

"Your mother gave you a Santee Sioux name?"

"It just so happens that my mother, Makawee, is a Santee Sioux."

"That makes you a half-breed as they say in your language."

"Or in my father's first language, métis."

"So do your mother's people live with the Santee Sioux who follow the game, or have they become farmers?"

"My mother's father is John Other Day. When he was younger, he was a trapper who traded with the French voyageurs. That's how he met my father who was a fur trader. But around fifteen years ago my grandfather settled down to farming. He also became a Christian."

"Christian farmers, eh? Well, my father is Little Crow, a Santee Sioux chief. We follow the wild game and hunt for our food, most of us would never farm, and we keep the traditional beliefs of our people."

Snowy Owl didn't let on that his father had at one time considered becoming a Christian but did not get baptized. He also did not let on that his father was well acquainted with white American society, its customs, laws, and form of government. In fact, he was embarrassed to think of his father once traveling to Washington City to negotiate a treaty with the Great White Father in which much of the Santee territory was ceded to the U.S. government in exchange for payments that were oftentimes late and almost always less than what was promised.

"Well, if you are going to shoot more arrows I better get out of range."

"No, you stay here, and I'll move to another place. You've probably scared away the deer with all your shouting anyway. Your grandfather's farm is probably close to my father's village. Next time you visit your grandfather, come visit me in Little Crow's village and I'll show you how Santee Sioux are supposed to live."

Robert felt that Snowy Owl's attitude was a bit haughty, but he did not pay it much mind.

"OK, I'd like to learn more about how you live."

Snowy Owl turned his back to Robert and began to walk away saying over his shoulder, "But I'm not interested in learning how you white people live."

Robert was a bit surprised by the rudeness of this comment but decided to let it go.

Later that day, Robert walked into his mother's kitchen where she was chopping vegetables. She saw the three fish in Robert's pail. "Oh, good job, Robert, you brought home tonight's supper! Unfortunately, your father came home empty-handed from his hunting trip. There will not be any venison anytime soon. I think your father is a lot better at trapping animals than he is hunting them with a musket," she said with a slight smile. Makawee was a beautiful woman, still youthful in appearance at thirty-one years of age.

"Oh Mom, you know that old muzzle-loaded musket is no good. It must be fifty years old! We need to get Father one of those modern musket rifles for better accuracy."

"That musket is very old, indeed. It was your father's father who owned that musket and used it in the war of 1812. Your father is quite attached to it, even though he is a trained gunsmith and could make a better musket himself. Perhaps he should try the bow. My people are quite good hunters with the bow and arrow."

"Speaking of bow and arrow, I was nearly hit by an arrow shot by a Santee Sioux boy today."

"What!!! I didn't think we had hostile Santee Sioux in these parts!"

"No, Mom. We were standing on opposite sides of a large bush on the riverbank. Without seeing me he simply mistook my rustling for a deer."

"You boys must learn to be careful! Did you get his name?"

"He said he was Snowy Owl, son of Chief Little Crow."

"Son of Chief Little Crow?" His mother looked a little concerned. "Was he friendly?"

"Kind of. He invited me to visit his village sometime."

"You must not visit that village without our permission. I will discuss this with your father."

At that moment, Robert's father, Henri Perrault, entered the house from the back door and walked up to his wife, and took her into his arms smiling. Henri was about thirty-nine years of age, with dark blonde hair and blue eyes. He stood about five feet and eleven inches tall and weighed about one hundred, eighty pounds, a robust mid-sized man. Makawee's eyes beamed as he hugged her. Henri truly loved his Indian wife, unlike some French trappers who traded furs for an Indian wife who would be useful for little more than menial labor and sex.

"Robert, it's time to chop some wood for the stove. Go out now and take care of that before supper."

"Yes, Pa!"

As soon as Robert left them to do his chore, Henri asked about Robert's encounter with Snowy Owl. Makawee had told him what Robert had said. Henri then asked about Little Crow, the Santee chief who was Snowy Owl's father.

"Is this the same Little Crow who was making some noise about white man's encroachment and destructive ways some time back? As I recall, we first heard about him being all riled up after the Grattan massacre in Nebraska Territory, and that seemed so distant and not with the Santee Sioux. Then most recently this past March, Little Crow got even more riled up about the Spirit Lake Massacre just over the border in Iowa. This time it was a renegade Santee chief, Scarlet Point (also known as Inkpaduta), who led a war party of fourteen braves in attacks on settlers, killing about forty of them and abducting four young women."

"Yes, it is the same Little Crow. And rumors have been in the wind that Little Crow harbored Scarlet Point's band when they came north into Minnesota. This could be a delicate situation. On one hand, Little Crow is known to have attended mission schools and he has attended church on occasion. He sometimes wears white American clothing and next to his teepee is an unfinished wooden house. He once traveled to Washington City to meet with the President and signed the treaty in 1858 that ceded land on the northern bank of the Minnesota River to the United States, and he has started to encourage his people to take up farming. But on the other hand, he is sympathetic with those in his tribe who believe that the Santee should return to their traditional ways and force the white man back to his home in the East. I sense a growing resentment and hostility toward white people among the Santee. I don't know if they will welcome Robert as a visitor to their village. But I think I understand Robert. I think that our son needs friendship and the white boys in this neighborhood tend to shun him because of me, his Indian mother. Naturally, he is considering the possibility of friends among the Santee, and he is just curious about how his Indian ancestors lived."

"I thought that you and your father were teaching Robert about his heritage. Isn't that enough?"

"My father has adopted the white man's ways by becoming a farmer, living in a wooden house, and worshipping Jesus. He can relate many aspects of the Santee culture to Robert, but not all of it. To thoroughly learn about the traditional ways of the Santee he would have to practically live with them."

"Well, I suppose we can let Robert be friends with this Santee boy, but I do have some concerns about Robert getting to know Little Crow and his warriors, though I think that Little Crow is probably a more reasonable man than most of his warriors."

"I am also a bit anxious, but Robert's grandfather would cancel out any ill effect of the warriors in Little Crow's village. My father is wise, having the wisdom of both the Santee and white man. We will just have to carefully question Robert about his interactions with this Santee boy and his friends."

"And his dealings with Little Crow and other adult warriors I would add."

⚎⚎⚎

CHAPTER TWO

Robert Perrault Visits Little Crow's Village

Robert woke up early and went right to work on his morning chores. The cows needed milking and the eggs needed to be collected and the chickens fed. Meanwhile, his mother was in the kitchen preparing breakfast for the family. Bacon and eggs were frying in a large cast-iron skillet filling the house with a delicious smell. After about fifteen minutes his mother called him in.

"Robert and Henri come to the table now, your breakfast is ready. Robert, you can return to your chores after breakfast."

The family sat down at the table but before they began to eat, they made the sign of the cross, and Henri offered up the meal prayer.

"Father God, please bless this meal, and all that it means. May the food nourish us, and this time spent with family enrich our lives. Most of all, may we always invite you into our home, and into our hearts. Amen."

"Why did you get up so early this morning, Robert?" his mother asked.

"I wanted to get my chores done so that I can ride over to Little Crow's village and visit Snowy Owl today. Remember, you said that I could go visit him if I got my chores done."

"OK, son. Remember to be respectful to the elders in the village. You know how your grandfather expects to be treated. Treat the elders in the village the same way."

"Keep in mind that the other boys will likely challenge you in various ways. That is part of the Santee way to prepare boys to become braves. If you are challenged to do something that is too dangerous, use your head. Don't do it."

"OK, Pa!"

ᏇᏇᏇᏇ

Robert selected Flora Belle from the stable. Flora Belle was a gentle mare who needed to get some exercise because she rarely got out to trot other than the Sunday trip to church when she pulled a buckboard wagon with her sister Nancy. Also in the stable were two fine Missouri mules named Claude and Samson. The mules were used only for farm tasks such as plowing and harvesting. The trip to Little Crow's village would take about ninety minutes at Flora Belle's comfortable trot at four miles per hour.

Robert found the village with no problem by following the Minnesota River. He guided Flora Belle to an open field where a large number of boys were playing a game which he would later find out, they called *baaga'adowe* («bump hips») a name they borrowed from the Ojibwa or Chippewa Indians who lived some miles east. Eastern Cherokee Indians called it *da-nah-wah'uwsdi* («little war»), and the Mohawks called it *begadwe* («little brother of war»). Today the game is known as lacrosse.

The figure on horseback caught the eye of Snowy Owl who then jogged over to Robert.

"Good, you chose a good day to visit. We are practicing bump hips in preparation for a game with the Ojibwa, who are rivals to the Santee. We have a quarrel with them, and our game should settle it without going to war. We also play this game to toughen ourselves up for combat in case we must go to war."

The other boys stopped their play and came over to surround Robert.

"What is a white boy doing here? Who invited him?" one
boy said with derision. Others grunted their agreement with
the sentiment. Snowy Owl held up his hand and said,

"I invited him here. And besides, half of his blood is Santee
Sioux. He's here to learn what it means to be a true Santee
Sioux."

This revelation placated Robert's would-be detractors. Just
then Snowy Owl's father, Little Crow, walked up to him and
grasped his shoulder indicating he wanted to speak to him
privately.

"A word with you son. This boy could be useful to us. Treat
him well. Test his mettle and his character, but don't put him in
any danger. He will need to feel that he can trust us."

Then Little Crow walked up to Robert and said to him,
"Greetings, Robert. I am Chief Little Crow. Snowy Owl says
your mother is Santee. Who among the Santee is her father?"

"Chief Little Crow, I am honored to meet you. My mother's
father is John Other Day. His farm is about a ten-minute ride
from here."

"I know your grandfather. He is an honorable man and those
of the Santee Sioux nation who follow the traditional ways were
sorry to lose him to the white man's way of life."

"Yes, sir. I understand. But I have heard only good things
about the Santee from him. He still deeply respects the Santee
way of life."

To that, the chief simply nodded and walked away.

Snowy Owl picked up the lacrosse stick left behind by Red
Falcon who was being carried from the field and handed it to
Robert. "Here take this. You will replace Red Falcon on my

team. Sit down and I will tell you the rules and object of the game."

As was their custom, the medicine men presided over the game. One would throw the ball high above the players, and all would try to catch it with their net pocket attached to the end of their stick. There were not any out-of-bounds and the field could extend a mile in length. For a game between rival tribes, hundreds of braves would play, and the game would last from dawn to dusk.

Little Crow observed the game appraisingly from a hill. Snowy Owl played aggressively and scored a two-point goal when he shot the ball and struck the stickball pole above the line at about eight feet. The area between chest height and eight feet is awarded one point when struck. And at the top of the pole was a totem of a sacred animal, such as a fish or eagle. When this totem was struck three points were awarded.

Robert hung back at first while he observed the game trying to pick up the rules and the pattern of play. Passing the ball was legal but was considered a trick. Dodging an opponent was viewed as a sign of cowardice. The players fought violently over the ball, justifying the game being called little brother of war or bump hips.

Little Crow noticed that Robert fell twice early during the game, but each time promptly got back on his feet. The third time he was knocked down he got a bloody nose and a cut on his lip, and he staggered to his feet. He crept over to the shade of a tree and collapsed heavily on the ground. A Santee girl ran over to him with a canteen and a rag. She wet the rag and washed his face and applied pressure to his nose and wound. Robert revived a bit and looked up at her in surprise. She was quite pretty with bright hazel eyes and a lighter complexion than most Santee.

"Sit still while I tend to you."

"Who are you?"

"I am Little Fox. That is my Ojibwa name translated into English. But my parents had named me Linda Marie."

"Your father is a white man?"

"Yes, he was a French fur trapper from St. Louis. We were visiting my mother's people on the other side of the river when a band of Santee braves attacked our village and killed many people, including my mother and father. I was just six years old when I was captured and made a slave."

"I am sorry to hear that! And to think that you have lived for what, nine years, as a captive to your parents' killers."

"Some of the Santee are nice to me, but not Little Crow's family."

"I would free you if I could. In fact, I want to talk to my grandfather about your situation. He knows a lot of people in this village."

"If you think it might help, please do!"

"By the way, thank you so much for helping me."

"It is the role of the women to tend to the wounded players."

"My lip must really be badly cut."

"It is. Let's just say you won't be kissing any pretty girls any time soon."

"That's a shame, I guess I'll just have to visit this village again when I'm all healed." Then Robert blushed when he realized what he had said.

Little Fox gave a faint smile and looked away to avoid his eyes. After a moment of silence, she said, "I'm surprised a white boy like you could last this long in this brutal game of bump hips."

"I'm a farm boy and fairly tough. But I am only half white. My father Henri Perrault is a French trader turned farmer and my mother is a Santee. I live over by the German settlement, New Ulm."

"A boy could walk that distance in two hours."

"Yes, but today I rode here on Flora Belle, our mare. Do you remember much of your father?"

"I remember that he had a red beard and that he would hold me on his lap and tell me stories about Jesus. I wish I could hear these stories again and more like them."

"Little Fox, I would be happy to tell you about Jesus and read the Bible to you."

"You would really? I would love that!"

Snowy Owl had left the game and was watching Little Fox and Robert, and he didn't like what he saw at all. He walked quickly up to them and shouted, "Little Fox you are done here, get away from him and go back to your mistress."

After she left, Snowy Owl half growled at Robert. "She will be my squaw someday. You better stay away from her."

"The son of the chief would marry a mixed-blood slave girl? That does not seem likely. What does Little Crow say about this?"

"He doesn't know anything about this. You'll just stay away from her if you know what is good for you!"

"I must return home now. Thank you for letting me play bump hips with your friends." Then Robert stood up unsteadily and walked to where he had left Flora Belle. He didn't wait for a response from Snowy Owl who stood with his arms folded and a scowl on his face.

On the ride home, Robert didn't think much at all about the game or his busted lip. The only image he had in his mind was the sweet smiling face of Little Fox.

ᏊᏊᏊ

CHAPTER THREE

Henri Designs a Special Rifle and
the Perrault Family Visits the Grandparents

It was dark by the time Robert rode Flora Belle through the gate of the Henri Perrault farm. As he arrived, Henri was saddling up Nancy to retrace Robert's path to Little Crow's village as his worried wife Makawee looked on.

"Henri, look-- this must be Robert now riding through the gate. He looks like he is slumping over in the saddle. He must have been hurt!" she said as she ran to intercept him.

"Robert, what happened? Were you attacked by bandits? Did the Santee boys hurt you? Oh, look at your face!"

Henri walked over and led Flora Belle to the stable after Robert slipped off.

"Did you get into a fight with a Santee boy?"

"No, Pa. I was learning how to play bump hips and got hit in the face."

"Bump hips is hardly a game. It is regarded as practice for war!" said Makawee.

"That's kind of what Snowy Owl said. The Santee were practicing before a big game with the Ojibwa to settle some dispute."

"Oh, these Sioux, all of them, the Dakota, the Lakota, the Yankton, all of them! They've always been so war-like!" said his mother with a sigh.

"Here, let's go inside and see how bad your wounds are."

"Oh, I'm fine Mom. A girl tended to my lip and bloody nose when I left the field"

"Was she pretty?" Makawee said with a smile.

"Yes, Mom she was pretty."

"I could tell because you are smiling!"

"Aw, Mommm!"

Henri could not resist saying, "This is a lot like how I met your mother, but my wounds were more serious!" And Henri lifted his shirt to show Robert his scars, left by an angry black bear.

"I encountered a black bear and her cubs in the woods and apparently, she thought I was too close to her cubs. She reared up and stood on her back legs and took a swipe at me, cutting right through my buckskin shirt. She was just about to bite me when I heard the crack of a rifle. The bears ran off, and I collapsed on the ground knocking myself out on a large flat rock. When I woke up, a pretty Indian girl was washing my wound. It turns out that it was your grandpa that shot that rifle. Finding me unconscious and bleeding, he improvised a travois and dragged me to his teepee, where his daughter Makawee took care of me. You know, I've always wanted to find that black bear!"

"To kill her?!"

"No, to thank her! Without her angry swipe at me I would have never met your mother!" And Henri drew his wife close to kiss her.

After the kiss, Makawee gently broke away from her husband's grasp and said, "Come with me now and I'll heat up the soup we had for dinner. I saved a couple of helpings for you."

The next day Robert found his father in his workshop drawing some kind of detailed picture on his draftsman's table. Henri's workshop was regarded as something of a local wonder. On two walls of this twelve-by-twelve-foot room hung his various tools for mechanical repairs, gunsmithing, and construction. On the other two walls, there were floor-to-ceiling bookshelves filled with books, mostly technical books but also some books on science and history. An autodidact in several subjects, Henri was drawing up plans for a rifle that was first invented in 1780 but that nearly everyone had forgotten.

"What are you designing, Pa?"

"This is a repeating air gun, such as Meriwether Lewis used in his expedition up the Missouri river with William Clark back in 1804. Meriwether Lewis bought this gun from the armory in Harpers Ferry, Virginia. It had been designed way back in 1780 by Girandoni in Vienna, Austria for use by the Austrian army against Napoleon. Compressed air shoots a .46 caliber ball with enough force to kill a deer at one hundred twenty-five yards. This magazine, (his pencil pointing to a tubular magazine on his plan), held up to twenty rounds. I'm going to see if I can improve on its design."

"Sounds great, but why didn't it catch on?"

"Well, there were three reasons that I suspect. One, it takes about fifteen hundred strokes of a hand pump to fill the reservoir. Two, the reservoirs are tricky to manufacture, and three, a small break in the reservoir could put the rifle out of commission. Added to all that is the simple fact that the air gun requires special training because it is so different from conventional weapons. But with the good Lord's help, I can develop an improved design that corrects these problems."

"Any special reason why you are reinventing this repeating rifle now?

"Well, your mother doesn't think I am successful enough hunting game with my musket."

"Pa, just how old is your musket, it was your father's musket, right?"

"You're right son, my musket is a 1795 Springfield, and your grandfather Robert used it in the war of 1812."

"Why not just buy a rifle? Why do you want to build one?"

"My accuracy would improve with a rifled barrel, but I still would have only one shot. I figure I need multiple shots to hit my target!"

"Like twenty shots, Pa?" said Robert, smiling.

"Yes, or maybe just nineteen," said a smiling father tousling his son's hair.

Henri didn't say what his real motivation was, but he was carefully preparing himself to defend his family and farm if the local Indians ever went on the warpath.

Early the next morning Henri and Makawee were lying in bed talking, and their conversation turned to Robert and his awakening interest in his Indian heritage.

"Perhaps we could arrange for Robert to stay with my parents for a few weeks so that he could feel more connected to his Santee heritage. I'm sure they would love to have him as a guest."

"That could be just what he needs, and your folks would give him a more balanced perspective on relations between whites and Indians than he would get from Little Crow."

"Can we load up the wagon after the corn harvest for a visit to my parents? Robert could stay with his grandparents for perhaps three weeks. Can you spare Robert from his farm duties for that long?"

"Yes, I think so. And if your father is still harvesting his corn, we can help him."

꧁꧂꧁꧂

CHAPTER FOUR

Grandfather Other Day Teaches
Robert Some Skills of the Sioux

John Other Day and his wife Roseanne happily welcomed their daughter and her family as their buckboard wagon pulled up to their home. Roseanne and Makawee ran to hug each other. "How long can you stay?" Roseanne and John said simultaneously.

Henri offered, "Well, we finished our corn harvest yesterday, so we can stay a few days to help you with yours if there's still work to be done. I asked our neighbors, Otto Krunkel and his family, to take care of our other animals."

"I'm only half done, so your help would be greatly appreciated!"

Henri, Robert, and John worked in the fields until dusk and were now returning in John's wagon back to the farmhouse. "Another day like today and we can be finished with your corn, John."

"That will be good, thank you both for helping me with this harvest!"

As they approached the farmhouse Henri said, "Robert, please take care of the wagon for us and unhitch the mules and water them, OK?"

"Sure thing, Pa!"

With Robert occupied, Henri drew aside his father-in-law.

"John, one of the reasons Makawee and I wanted to have Robert visit you is that he has made friends of sorts with Snowy Owl, son of Little Crow. We think that he is simply interested in learning about the Santee way of life, but there is the risk of Little Crow's influence."

John's face showed concern when he said, "Well, that is something of a cause for concern. I don't know Snowy Owl, but Little Crow has been making a lot of noise about the encroachment of white men on Indian land. He might be just waiting for the right moment to launch an attack on the white settlements in this part of Minnesota. And there is talk, just talk mind you, that he has given haven to those Sioux who were responsible for the Spirit Lake massacre some months back."

"Do you think the local Santee, Little Crow's band, in particular, are thinking of war?"

"Henri, that's exactly what I'm thinking about. If crops do not get any better soon, or if the deer and other game become even more scarce, we could be in trouble. Listen, Henri. I'll keep Robert here for a few weeks. I'll teach him archery, how to build a canoe, how to set up a teepee, how to track wild game, and other skills of the Santee. And his grandmother will likely want to remind him of his Christian faith and how that should guide his behavior, and contrast that with the way of the Santee."

"That all sounds fine to me, John. Robert will be in good hands, thank you!"

🦀🦀🦀

Two days passed and the corn harvest was now complete giving John Other Day some time to teach Robert about archery. John had first taught Robert about how to make a bow and arrows starting with the right kind of wood. Then he coached

Robert on the principles of archery and set him to practice shooting arrows at a target set back about sixty feet.

"OK, Robert. Let's practice with the target at this distance until your accuracy improves, then we'll move back another ten feet from the target."

Just then, Makawee walked over with her own bow and quiver of arrows. "I see that you saved these for me, Father."

"Yes, and I don't know why, to be honest! I guess it's hard for me to throw away reminders of you."

"That's sweet of you, Father. Can I test my skills with the bow? Robert, may I have a turn?"

"Sure thing, Mom."

Makawee appeared like she wanted to shoot from where she was standing, which was about ten feet back from Robert. Realizing this, Robert stepped away from the line of fire. Makawee then quickly launched five arrows and hit the smallest circle on the target four times. The fifth shot was only an inch away.

John Other Day smiled at his daughter's performance. And Robert simply said "Wow!"

Makawee said, "It's nice to know I can still hit the target. When I was your age, Robert, I was better at this than most of the boys. It drove them crazy with envy."

"Your mother is being modest. She was actually better than all of the boys!

"Which did not make me popular with them because they did not want to lose to a girl!"

"Yes, and if I had not persuaded that bear to take a swipe at Henri, you might still be without a husband!"

"Father, stop that!" said Makawee smiling.

"Well, it looks like I'll need a lot of practice before I am as good as you, Mom!"

"Show me now how well you handle your bow."

Robert complied and shot five arrows, all of them landing in the third ring.

"Robert, this is very good for a beginner, just keep practicing."

And so, Robert practiced for many hours over several weeks thinking of the day when he would have to prove his worth to the Santee.

ᏩᏩᏩ

Robert stayed with his grandparents for four weeks, as it turned out, to give his grandfather more time to teach Robert how to build a dugout canoe, set up a teepee, and other skills shared by the Sioux tribes. This morning Robert was in the farmyard practicing his archery shooting at a target nailed to the side of the barn. His concentration was broken by his grandmother's call from the back door of the farmhouse. "Robert, please come here, there is someone here I want you to meet." Robert said, "Yes, Ma'am" and set down his bow and arrows, and jogged over to the farmhouse where his grandmother was waiting.

Robert followed his grandmother into the kitchen and was surprised to see that Little Fox was standing there!

"Robert, I want you to meet Little Fox, who lives with the Santee Sioux in Little Crow's village."

Little Fox extended her hand and Robert grasped it and unconsciously lingered there with it.

"Grandmother, Little Fox and I actually met some weeks ago. She was the girl who..."

"Took care of him when he got hurt playing bump hips," said Little Fox, finishing his sentence.

"Little Fox came here for some of our produce. Until recently, this band of the Santee was mostly nomadic and are just now learning agriculture so they must trade for their fruits and vegetables. Our farm must look like a bountiful source!"

"It really is wonderful, Grandmother Roseanne! It reminds me of my mother's garden plot in our Ojibwa village. You see, I am not Santee. My mother was Ojibwa, and my father was French. Both mother and father were killed when the Santee raided our village and killed many people. I was just six years old."

"Oh no, that is so sad! Did a nice Santee family adopt you?

"Running Deer and his wife, Kimimela, adopted me, but they don't treat me like a daughter. I am essentially a slave girl. No one is surprised by this because Running Deer is the brother of Chief Little Crow, and both brothers are known for their hatred of the Ojibwa."

"Well, precious daughter (may I call you that?), I too had an Ojibwa mother and a white father. He was an English soldier in the war of 1812 and a lay Methodist preacher who chose to stay in America rather than return to England with his regiment."

Robert was taken aback by this information, "Grandmother, did you mean to say that you are not Sioux at all, but Ojibwa and not even all Ojibwa but half white? Then you are a half-breed like me!"

Grandmother smiled tilting her head and said, "Yes, but a polite way to say that is that I have a mixed heritage or mixed ancestry. And by the way, taken altogether, this means that you are three-eighths Indian and five-eighths white (or European). So, you are more white than Indian!"

Robert pulled out a chair at the kitchen table and sat down with a plop. "This kind of changes the way I've been thinking about myself. I'm not sure who or what I am supposed to be.

Am I an Indian or am I white? Neither white people nor Indians have fully accepted me."

With a gentle shake of her head Grandmother said, "Robert, you should first identify yourself as a Christian, and not be concerned with being white or Indian. Jesus accepts you the way you are."

"Oh, I know Grandmother. What you say is true. It's just that I don't have any real friends."

Little Fox jumped in to say, "You have me as your friend! Grandmother, would it be all right for us to meet here at your farm a few times a month? I can get away from the village a couple of times during the week."

Grandmother responded, "That would be fine by me, Little Fox! Robert, you could ride Flora Belle here after your chores. I'm sure your father and mother can spare you some time each week."

"Yes, I like this idea a lot!" said Robert.

"Now Little Fox, can you spend some more time with us now, or do you need to get back to the village?"

"I can stay for another hour or so!"

"Good, then I'll read the two of you some of the Bible as you requested. Robert, please take your friend to the front porch, and I'll be with you in a few minutes after I fix us some lemonade."

Robert and Little Fox walked to the front porch and sat down on the steps. Little Fox turned to Robert and said with a smile, "Your lip has healed well. Then hesitatingly, "So if you want to kiss me..." And when Robert kissed this beautiful girl, he could have floated up to the clouds.

඿඿඿

CHAPTER FIVE

Robert Wins an Archery Contest

Despite the epiphany Robert had about his ethnic heritage, that he was more white or European than he was Indian, Robert still sought acceptance and approval from the Santee boys his age at Little Crow's village. But the Santee boys would not be won over easily. They weren't rude or mean in their interactions with him, but most were not warm and welcoming either. Although Robert felt some kinship with them, they only saw a white boy, because it was easy to forget that he had a Santee mother. It did not help Robert's situation any that relations of the Santee with the white settler community were strained and growing worse.

Robert continued to visit Little Crow's village and tried to fit in by growing his hair long and tying it back like the Indian boys. He even wore buckskins his mother made for him, but he still did not win universal acceptance. Instead, he noticed that the Santee boys seemed to be falling into one of two groups. One group was accepting and after a while seemed to overlook his whiteness. They would talk and joke with him, and even invite him to their family teepee where he might share a meal with them. The second group of boys seemed uneasy with him and didn't even greet him when he showed up for an archery contest or a game of bump hips. If he got any response at all from these boys, it was a grunt as they walked away. And with time it seemed that the division between these two groups of boys was growing sharper, especially as Robert became more and more proficient in archery and bump hips.

One day almost a year after Robert first met Snowy Owl, there was an impromptu archery contest and the competition narrowed down to two boys for first place, Snowy Owl and Robert. Snowy Owl could barely hide his irritation that a half-breed might win this contest.

Snowy Owl stepped up to take his turn at the target and with his three shots, his arrows made a tight triangle around the bull's eye. "Ha! You can't possibly beat that, half-breed!"

It bothered Robert some that Snowy Owl would not address him by his name anymore, always using this disparaging label instead, but he squelched those emotions and stepped up to aim and shoot. His first arrow landed in the middle of the triangle made by Snowy Owl and the boys looking on whooped in delight! This really disturbed Snowy Owl and he scowled as he folded his arms.

Robert's next two arrows landed next to Snowy Owl's arrows and just as close to the center.

Snowy Owl could not restrain himself and ran up to the target to check for himself. As he swung around back to the crowd to declare himself the winner, his father Chief Little Crow stepped in and spoke up, "Robert, the grandson of John Other Day, has won this contest!"

By this time adult warriors had joined the crowd of onlookers, and some looked at Snowy Owl with mild scorn on their faces. Snowy Owl was an excellent archer but a poor sportsman. His reaction to his narrow loss was an embarrassment.

Robert thought it would be a good time to return home and avoid a confrontation with Snowy Owl. As he approached the tree where he had tied Flora Belle, Little Fox ran up to him and hugged him, bouncing with delight over his victory. Robert smiled and hugged her back. But Snowy Owl furtively looked on some fifty yards away, and he seethed with anger and jealousy.

ᑕᑕᑕ

CHAPTER SIX

Vision Quest

When Robert last visited the Santee village some of the friendlier Santee boys spoke of the vision quests that they went on during the past year. Robert was fascinated and wanted to learn more.

"Do you mean to say that you have never heard of a vision quest before? How old are you? Sixteen, right? Then you are overdue." This came from Silver Wolf, probably Robert's best friend among the Santee.

"To have a vision quest you must go to some isolated place alone. You may have a weapon to defend yourself against a bear, wolf, or badger; but you cannot have food. You must stay awake and pray to Wakan Tanka, the Great Spirit. He is all that is holy and mysterious. He is the creator of the universe, and everything that has life lives within him. The Sun, the Moon, the Stars, the Earth, all animals, and the human soul – these are all manifestations of the Wakan Tanka."

"So how long does a person have to wait before a vision comes to him, and what happens in a vision?"

"The Great Spirit may come at any time during the quest. But some boys must wait four days or more. And what happens in the vision depends on what the Great Spirit wants the boy to see. You will experience a symbolic death and rebirth and gain a vision of your guardian spirit or spirit animal that becomes your guide in life. This guardian spirit might also give you your new songs and rituals that you may use to help you through challenging and difficult times."

After hearing this, Robert decided that this vision quest could be just the thing he needs to find his direction in life, whether Indian or white, and he planned to talk with his parents about it.

When he returned home, he was pleasantly surprised to see that his grandparents were visiting his family. He found his parents and grandparents talking on the front porch.

"I have something I want to discuss with you, all of you."

Looking at the others for their reaction, Henri said, "Well, go ahead and let us know what is on your mind, son."

"I was talking to Silver Wolf about the vision quest. I think I would like to try this myself."

Henri looked to John who said, "Traditionally this is a time when a young man isolates himself from other humans in some remote place and fasts and prays to Wakan Tanka, the Great Spirit, for a vision of what direction he should take in his life. I went on a vision quest when I was about fourteen. This was before I became a Christian and up to that point, I had believed that Wakan Tanka was the one true Great Spirit. But you, Robert, are you not a believer in God of the Bible and his son, Jesus, together with the Holy Spirit?"

"Grandfather, I always will be a Christian, I will never abandon my faith. So, I was thinking I should fast and pray to God during my vision quest."

"In the New Testament the gospel speaks of how Jesus went into the wilderness and fasted and prayed for forty days, and various times during his ministry he went off to a secluded place away from others and prayed to his father. And so, I would say there is a precedent for what you want to do, Robert, in the Bible itself," offered Henri.

"Robert, please give us some time now to discuss this idea of a vision quest privately. Please leave us for now, and I will get you when we are ready for you," said Makawee.

The adults then discussed the idea and decided that it would be a good thing for Robert to seek God's guidance in this manner. Then Makawee brought Robert back to where the adults were sitting. Henri spoke for the adults, "We think that this vision quest would be a good thing for you to do. If you like, we'll help you choose a place for your vigil and make other plans tomorrow morning. But for now, say goodbye to your grandparents because they need to return home before it gets dark."

☙☙☙☙

As Robert completed his chores the next morning, Henri emerged from his workshop and waved Robert over to join him inside. "Robert, I know that your birthday is not for another two weeks, but I have something for you that you will want to carry with you on your vision quest. Come here and see!"

Once inside, his father handed him a large cardboard box. It was heavier than what Robert was expecting, and when he opened it, he realized why. The box held a Colt 1851 Navy revolving pistol and a leather holster. There was also a detachable wooden stock which when attached, would steady the weapon, and improve accuracy. Robert was speechless with this gift. He had not expected anything like this.

"I purchased a gun and holster for myself as well. Mr. Krunkel, a fine leather craftsman as well as a farmer, made these. Well, let's try on the holster. That's right, now secure the holster to your thigh with that leather string on the bottom. Not too tight, remember that its purpose is to enable you to quickly draw your gun without your holster shifting on you. You don't want it so tight that it restricts your leg motion."

"Thanks, Pa! But why buy guns now? Are you expecting trouble from the Santee?"

"To be honest, I am somewhat anxious about the Santee. If the crops don't produce and the wild game doesn't improve, we can expect trouble. But a more immediate need is something for self-protection during your vision quest. You will need something handier than an old musket. It probably will not happen, but you want to be prepared against bear, wolf, wildcat, or coyote out there on your own."

Then father and son went on the buckboard wagon to an isolated spot where they could practice firing their Colt 1851 revolvers. Henri was much more accurate than Robert expected him to be, and he was knowledgeable and able to instruct Robert on the art of shooting, coaching him on the essentials of aiming using sight alignment and sight picture, and the essentials of hold control, breath control, trigger control, and follow-through. Robert learned quickly and noted how much more accurately he could shoot using the wooden shoulder stock and the sights on the barrel.

Robert rose early the next morning and performed his usual chores. Afterward, he had a big breakfast with his parents. Then he packed his backpack with his pup tent, a thick wool sweater, canteen, matches, a hand ax, and a folding shovel for digging a fire pit. On his person, he had his holster and Colt 1851, and a broad-brimmed leather hat. After a hug from his mother and a handshake from his father, Robert set off on foot. He told his parents he would set up camp on a wooded hillside about two miles away.

Finding a suitable place to set camp, Robert set up his pup tent and sat down at its entrance. It was now late September, and the temperature could dip down into the forties after sunset, but Robert was prepared with a heavy sweater. The clouds in the sky indicated that rain was likely later in the day, so he was glad he had brought the pup tent. He was all for the experience of silence and prayer, but he did not think he needed to be cold and wet to achieve the spiritual connection he sought. As the evening approached, Robert dug out a shallow pit for his campfire and gathered twigs and larger dry branches for fuel for the fire. Then after lighting the fire, he sat back and started his prayers and meditation.

"Father God, creator of both heaven and earth, and all its creatures, there is none like you. There is no God but you. You are slow to anger and quick to forgive. I know that I have failed you in so many ways. I have not obeyed you in all things, I have failed by not doing what I should have done, and by doing things I should not have done. I have not shared my faith with my Indian friends because I am weak and fearful, fearful of being rejected by the Santee boys. I have worked hard to acquire the skills of the Santee but have not shared what I know to be true about you Lord. Please give me the courage to be a better witness.

I thank you Lord for all that you have given me in this life. Wonderful parents and grandparents who have loved me and taught me so many things. I thank you for our farm and its success, for all good things come from you, Lord. Thank you for Little Fox, whom I love. If she is the girl I should marry, please make that clear. In the meantime, please protect Little Fox from all harm and help my family to find a way to free her from those who have enslaved her, with no kindness or love for these past nine years.

Dear Lord, please show me the way I should go. Am I to live as an Indian or as a white settler? Should I go west, stay here, or go back east? Should I become a farmer, gunsmith, carpenter, or something else? Show me which road I should take."

As he finished his prayer, Robert sat still trying to clear his mind and heart and listen to God. As the night progressed, the weather grew cold, and a light rain began to fall. He sat at the entrance to his tent listening to the night sounds of the forest. An owl hooted and an animal of some species walked through the brush, crunching some fallen leaves. Too small to be a bear, was it a fox, coyote, wolf, or bobcat? The moonlight flashed on the animal's eyes, and they reflected as green lights. Robert decided it was a bobcat, and touched the handle of his Colt 1851, assuring himself that it was handy.

The next day was a repeat of the first day. Since it looked like it would rain again and get cold, Robert dug a better fire pit and laid in it a foundation of stones. Then he recalled what his grandfather taught him about a self-feeding fire. Robert was fortunate to find a thick branch that had broken from a tree. With his ax, he chopped that branch into logs and used smaller branches to build a type of slanting rack on either side of the campfire. From the side, it looked like a V-shaped contraption that allowed logs to roll down into the fire as the bottom log was burned through. Under the bottom log, Robert had placed kindling that he had saved in his tent. Then he lit the kindling. The thick logs would protect the underlying fire from the rain. This project took up much of the day. Then tired and hungry, Robert sat at the entrance of his tent as the sunset came.

Again, he prayed and revealed the deep concerns of his mind and heart, and he sat and listened. He sat up much of the night being warmed by the fire, then it began to rain. He retreated to his pup tent and wrapped a wool blanket around himself to keep warm. As the hours wore on, Robert fought to keep awake. But eventually, despite his best efforts, he fell asleep. And then the dreams began.

Robert looked up and saw what appeared to be a young man dressed in a white robe or tunic sitting in his tent. He was illuminated by some strange inner source. Around his waist there appeared to be a golden belt. The young man smiled as Robert looked on in confusion. After some seconds Robert found his voice, "Who are you? And what are you doing in my tent? Are you a *wakanpi, a spirit who controls events on earth?"*

"Greetings Robert! Do not be afraid; I am only a messenger from God. There is no such thing as a *wakanpi*. Robert, God has heard your prayers and has sent me to tell you that he has plans for you, plans to prosper you and not to harm you, plans to give you hope and a future. Soon you will experience a period of tumult, war, and suffering. But you and your family will be protected and come through this trial unscathed. As for Little Fox, do not be afraid to take her as your wife. The Holy Spirit is with her. But wait for the right time for marriage. The two of you will know when the time is right."

The messenger began to fade away and Robert said, "Wait, should I go the way of the white man, or the Indian?"

The messenger simply smiled and said, "For now sleep. More will be revealed to you."

Thus, Robert slept only to have another dream or vision (he could not tell the difference) interrupt his sleep. This time Robert found himself walking on a dusty dry road with a group of twelve oddly dressed men and a few women. They were following a man perhaps in his early thirties and those around him were listening intently to what he was saying. People around Robert were singing a hymn of sorts. The tune was unlike anything Robert had heard before, but the words reminded him of a psalm in the Bible. After walking some miles in the heat of the day, Robert worked up the courage and ran up to the man leading the procession, whom the others were addressing as Yeshua. Yeshua smiled when he saw Robert and put his hand on his shoulder. "Greetings Robert, peace be with you. Do you know who I am and where we are going?"

"Are you Jesus the son of God, my Lord and Savior? And are we headed to Jerusalem?"

The man smiled and said, "Yes, what you say is true. Now listen, we are approaching Jerusalem and coming to Bethphage on the Mount of Olives, I am sending you and John to go ahead of us to the village. As you arrive there, at once you will find a donkey tied to a hitching post, with her colt by her. Untie them and bring them to me. If anyone says anything to you, say that the Lord needs them, and he will send them back right away."

"Yes, my Lord!" And as Robert turned, he saw a young man, perhaps a little older than himself, who said, "My name is John. Let's leave now and bring back the animals our Lord has requested."

"How long have you known Jesus?" Robert asked John.

"I met Jesus about three years ago when he was just starting his public ministry. How long have you known Jesus?"

"I just met him today."

"That's odd. It seemed like he has known you all your life!"

"Wait, how can it be that you can speak English?"

"What is English? You and I are speaking Aramaic. Your question is most puzzling!"

They found the animals where Jesus said they would find them and walked them back to Jesus.

"Thank you, Robert and John. Now, Robert, you should return home. Remind Makawee, Henri, Roseanne, John, and Little Fox that I love them dearly. And Robert, know this: there are only two types of people in the world. Those who believe and so are saved, and those who don't believe and so are lost. It does not matter whether you are a white settler or Indian, you are precious to me. Go and live your life following me. As for your "spirit animal," just remember this humble donkey who carried the Son of Man into Jerusalem."

Robert smiled and wanted to say something but felt himself being drawn back. Then he woke up and found himself back in his pup tent. He reached into his bag and found his canteen. He was thirsty after being in that desert. Then reaching into his bag again, he found a barley loaf, which he didn't remember putting there. With his vision completed, he ate the barley loaf and fell back asleep.

The next morning Henri and Makawee were sitting at the kitchen table when Robert arrived home from his vision quest.

"Was your vision quest successful?" Makawee asked.

"Yes, it was quite successful. I've never experienced anything like this before in my life!"

Henri asked, "Can you describe your vision for us?"

Then Robert told them about the two visions, leaving out the part about Little Fox because he was embarrassed to let them know he was so seriously in love with her.

"Oh my, that must have been quite an experience! You must be really hungry now; I'll make you a big breakfast."

"Thanks, Mom! By the way, that barley loaf you packed for me was just what I needed," said Robert as he headed to his room to change out of his dirty and smoky clothes. He was singing the strange hymn he learned on his walk to Jerusalem.

Then with a puzzled expression, Makawee said to Henri, "I didn't pack a barley loaf for him. I don't even have barley flour to bake such a loaf." And Makawee and Henri just sat there staring at each other in wonderment.

☙☙☙

CHAPTER SEVEN

John Other Day Tries to Get
Little Fox Released from Bondage

Robert and Little Fox were now seventeen years old. For more than a year Little Fox had been visiting Roseanne Other Day, Robert's grandmother at the Other Day farm, and a great fondness had grown between the two women. One day Little Fox appeared at Roseanne's door with tears in her eyes. When Roseanne opened the door, Little Fox collapsed into her arms.

"Oh, my goodness, Little Fox, what is wrong?" Little Fox could hardly speak for all her sobbing and Roseanne sat with her and attempted to comfort her. After some minutes of this, Little Fox was able to tell Roseanne what had happened to her.

"This morning as I went to the river to fetch some water for my mistress, a man grabbed me and forced me to the ground. There was no one else there, and he held his hand over my mouth so that I could not scream for help. Then he, he...put his hand in my dress... Before he could do anything else, Little Crow appeared and told him to get off me."

"The man obeyed the chief but lied to him and said that I had invited him to touch me but then changed my mind. The chief believed him, and the man went unpunished. Before he left me, Little Crow said that I should not flirt with men if I didn't want to have sex with them!"

Roseanne, I haven't flirted with any man or boy in the village. I am innocent!"

"I know you are, precious child. Tonight, you will stay with us in this house. We will protect you. Do you know the name of the man who assaulted you?"

"Yes, the chief called him Roaring Cloud."

When John Other Day came in from his work in the field that afternoon, Roseanne told him about the assault on Little Fox. John was deeply disturbed by this development and resolved that he had to help Little Fox escape from her horrid living conditions. She had not been treated with kindness and truly adopted into a Santee family as honor would proscribe. Instead, she had been kept as a slave doing menial work, and now she was not safe from lusty men in the village.

"Roseanne, did Little Fox mention the name of her attacker?"

"Yes, she said she heard Chief Little Crow call him Roaring Cloud."

"Roaring Cloud, son of Inkpaduta!" John rose quickly from his kitchen chair and paced around the room. "Inkpaduta is the name of that renegade who along with his braves from another band, killed all those settlers in the Spirit Lake region last winter. I suspected that they were hiding with Little Crow."

John Other Day grabbed an apple from a bowl on the table then excused himself and headed to his corral. Roseanne called out to him from the back door,

"John, where are you going, and what are you going to do?"

"Don't worry Roseanne, I am just considering what I might give Little Crow in exchange for Little Fox."And I think I have just the right thing," he said as he approached the corral.

"What is it, John?"

"This beautiful stallion, Black Lightning. The Santee value horses more than any other living thing!"

Then Roseanne felt both sadness and hope at the same time. Sadness that her husband would have to lose the animal he loved the most and hope that Little Fox might be freed from her loveless and dangerous situation and become her daughter. The depth of her heartache for this girl could not be described in words.

After giving the horse the treat, John returned to the house and said, "Tomorrow morning at first light I will take Black Lightning to the Santee village and trade the stallion for this girl."

"You are not planning to return Little Fox to that horrid village, are you John?"

"No, not unless I am forced to. If Little Crow will not trade and wants the girl back, then at least I want his assurances that she will be protected. And if he will not make any promises then I will tell him that the U.S. Army at Fort Ridgely would be most interested in the half-white girl he is keeping as his brother's slave. Be assured that I will not rest until Little Fox is freed."

༄ༀ༄ༀ

The next morning John Other Day rode his draft horse with Black Lightning in tow to Little Crow's village. He dismounted and led the horses to the center of the village. Some persons looked up in surprise, for John was wearing settlers' clothes, but others quickly recognized him as a returning brother, with some of the older ones greeting him like a long-lost relative. Two young braves stopped John and asked him his business. John replied, "I am John Other Day and I am here to discuss a trade with Chief Little Crow."

"Wait here. We will bring him to you."

A few minutes later Little Crow walked over to where John was waiting. "John Other Day, I understand that you came here to trade."

"Yes, I want to request that you release an Ojibwa girl, Little Fox, from her bondage. My wife loves her and would be a good mother to her. I am prepared to trade this beautiful stallion for the girl."

"I know this Little Fox. She has caught the eye of my braves with her beauty and the way she walks. This girl has great value to me. If you want her, then you should come back with two stallions of this quality."

"Chief Little Crow, Black Lightning here, is a prized stallion. He is worth ten ordinary horses! Only a rich man would have two horses of this quality!"

"So, you are not a rich man? You are said to have a prospering farm, but apparently, it has not made you rich. I'll tell you what you can do. In a few days, several braves will be going with me to hunt buffalo. You are invited to come with us. Any buffalo you kill you can give to me along with this stallion. I would expect two kills. Then you may have Little Fox. You may keep Little Fox at your farm for two more days. Then I will send some braves to your farm to take her back to the village. She will be needed to help the other women prepare provisions for our trip and then help with processing the buffalo hides and meat, so she will be going on the hunting trip along with some other women. And you may keep your stallion in the meantime. You will need a strong swift horse for the hunt."

"Chief, I want your guarantee that the girl will be safe from the sexual advances of your braves. She is not ready to become anyone's wife."

"I will tell her master, my brother, to watch over her. Do not worry."

As John was leaving the village, Inkpaduta and Roaring Cloud came up to Chief Little Crow. With a scornful sneer Roaring Cloud said, "When he returns with the girl I desire, I should kill him and take both the beautiful stallion and the girl from him."

The chief turned and looked at him with a raised eyebrow and said, "You are a fool! You would not win a fair fight with this man John Other Day. As a younger man, he was a formidable warrior, and I don't believe he has lost any of his strength or courage. You may have killed more men than he has, but you killed unarmed white farmers, their wives, and children. There is no honor in that kind of killing."

"My father and I did what needed to be done! Those whites were defiling our sacred land and lake."

"Did you think that your violence would not be answered with violence?"

⚭⚭⚭

John Other Day was not at all pleased with the outcome of his attempt to trade for Little Fox's freedom. Roseanne noticed him returning and noted that he still had the stallion with him. John decided to portray his agreement with Little Crow in the best possible light, but this did nothing to soothe Roseanne's anxiety. "You mean in two days Santee braves will come to take Little Fox back to the village?"

"Yes, Roseanne. But I will be following them."

"And both you and Little Fox will be going on the buffalo hunt? For how many days?"

"After I shoot and kill two buffalo for Chief Little Crow, I will return as soon as possible. But I won't leave without Little Fox. Listen, tomorrow let us visit Makawee and her men, Henri and Robert. I want Robert to come with me on this hunting trip. He might kill a buffalo before I do, and I think it would be better to have a companion on this potentially dangerous hunt."

"Now, Robert too? Oh, this just keeps getting better and better," said Roseanne with a rare edge of sarcasm in her voice. "Oh, forgive me Lord! Help me to trust in you and not be anxious!"

Early the next morning John, Roseanne, and Little Fox set out for the Perrault farm on John's buckboard wagon. John took the precaution of having Black Lightning in tow rather than leave him unguarded and susceptible to theft. On the way, they ran into Robert on Flora Belle.

"Hey, this is a surprise! I was going to your farm for a visit!" said Robert.

"But we decided to visit your parents and you," said Roseanne.

"I need to speak with your father and mother about some important business that affects all of us, Robert," said John.

What sort of business might that be, grandfather?"

"Robert, just wait until we get to your father's farm, and we'll discuss it all together."

"Good morning, Little Fox!"

"Good morning, Robert!" she said with a smile that caused his heart to skip a beat, and when she thought Robert's grandparents weren't looking, she blew him a kiss.

☙❧☙❧

Makawee was quite happy to meet Little Fox and said, "So now I see why Robert has wanted to visit his grandparents every other day!"

Little Fox just blushed and said, "Robert told me that his mother was beautiful, and I see now that he was not exaggerating! I am so happy to meet you."

After all the greetings, hugs, and small talk, John asked the youngsters to go for a walk and give the adults some privacy. Then the four adults sat down at the kitchen table and John related how he and Roseanne wanted to help Little Fox escape the loveless and now dangerous situation she had at the Santee village and how they wanted to adopt Little Fox. John also related his story with Little Crow, and how he would need to not only give Little Crow his prize stallion, Black Lightning, but also two buffalo.

"John, would Little Crow accept two ordinary Holsteins in place of two buffalo? They are far easier to come by."

"No, it's far more than the meat and the hide that he wants. He wants to make me work and sweat for this trade. Which I am willing to do because this girl's life means so much more to us."

"So, Father, do you need Henri to come along on this hunt?"

"No, I believe the Lord is leading me to bring Robert. Henri would not be accepted because he is a white man, but Robert has become a familiar figure in Little Crow's village. Also, Little Crow requires his hunters to kill the buffalo with arrows and spears as in the old days. Robert is proficient with the bow now."

Makawee's anxiety was in danger of overwhelming her, "Father, will you promise to stay close to Robert and watch over him?"

"I promise to keep him close to me at all times."

"Henri, what do you think about this?"

"I think that we will have to trust in God and your father for their safety and success. The cause is good, and I believe it is following God's will. If Little Fox is ever to be freed from her bondage, we must do this." The four adults looked at each other and nodded in agreement. Then Roseanne offered up a prayer to which everyone said "amen."

♋♋♋

CHAPTER EIGHT

The Buffalo Hunt

On the first day of preparation for the buffalo hunt, three Santee braves came to John Other Day's farm. They were on horseback and looked annoyed as if the task they were sent on was beneath them. They rode up to where John and Robert were packing materials on John's buckboard wagon. The three braves were the two sons of Inkpaduta, Roaring Cloud and Black Eagle, and Snowy Owl. Roaring Cloud spoke for them, "We are here to fetch the girl, Little Fox. Bring her to us now."

"I can't. She isn't here. Robert and I are going now to fetch her once we load up this wagon with our supplies. Then we will bring her with us to Little Crow's village."

"That is not what Little Crow told us to do. Old man, you hand her over to us now or you will take a beating."

Snowy Owl said to Roaring Cloud, "Listen, Roaring Cloud, the man said the girl isn't here."

"He is lying! Little Crow said she would be here."

"So, you are Roaring Cloud! Your reputation precedes you."

Roaring Cloud spat, dismounted quickly, and made like he was going to invade John's house; but he came too close to John Other Day. John grabbed him and, in a flash, threw him on the ground, knocking the wind out of the over-confident brave. Robert looked on in shock!

Then as Roaring Cloud scrambled to his feet, Black Eagle dismounted and ran to stand behind John's back. Robert realized

53

what was about to happen. Fortunately, he was wearing his holster. He withdrew his revolver and shot once in the air.

"That was just a warning shot! You just get back on your ponies and hightail it back to your village."

"Would you really shoot us boy?" Roaring Cloud said with a sneer.

"I would. You had better believe I would shoot you in defense of family or property."

Snowy Owl looked on with amazement at the half-breed boy. He was showing more strength and courage than he would have imagined. Snowy Owl said, "I believe him! I know this boy. He is proficient with both bow and gun. Let's just leave now, and I'll tell my father there had been a change in plans. Come on, get back on your ponies and let's get out of here."

"This isn't over, old man!" Roaring Cloud growled at John.

"If it isn't over, I know how it will end."

Without saying another word, the three Santee men galloped away.

"Robert, were you really prepared to shoot a man?"

"Grandfather, you didn't see the man behind you reaching for his knife! Yes, I was ready to kill a man if that prevented you from being killed."

John sighed and said "Then you did the right thing. But I would want to spare you the experience of killing another human being. Shamefully, some Santee warriors will kill for pleasure, but they are filled with the destroyer of souls. But we must never learn to enjoy killing for revenge or any other reason we might conjure up to justify our sin."

John and Robert finished packing up the buckboard wagon and began the trip to the Perrault farm. Roseanne was already staying at the Perrault's along with Little Fox.

When they pulled into the Perrault farm Little Fox came running up to the wagon. Robert jumped down and accepted Little Fox's hug and kiss. Roseanne and Makawee looked on and smiled. "They are definitely two young lovers, not brother and sister!" said Roseanne.

"I don't think Robert could have found a nicer or sweeter girl!" said Makawee.

"Nor could have Little Fox found a finer young man," responded Roseanne.

Little Fox did not have a change of clothing with her when she escaped to Roseanne's house, but Roseanne still had some Sioux clothing that had belonged to Makawee when she was a teenager. She gave these to Little Fox so that she could change out of soiled clothing on the hunt. She also made her an apron to wear during the messy part of field dressing the buffalo carcass. The family gathered together in a circle and said a prayer for protection for John, Robert, and Little Fox during the buffalo hunt; then the three of them got on the buckboard wagon and left for Little Crow's village.

When they arrived at Little Crow's village, Little Fox's masters, Running Deer, and his wife, Kimimela, noticed the buckboard wagon and walked over to pick up their slave girl. Running Deer was angry and said, "Wichinjcala (girl), your work has been waiting for you. Go now to our teepee and wait for us there, and your mistress will tell you what to do in preparation for the buffalo hunt." Then looking at John, "So, you are John Other Day. I remember you from your warrior days. Do you want to acquire Little Fox as your slave or is it as your daughter? As she is the daughter of an Ojibwa woman and a wasichu (white man) she is not worth much except as a servant and concubine. Well, my brother Little Crow has told you the price."

"Yes, we shall provide two buffalo carcasses and this black stallion in exchange for the girl. In the meantime, my grandson and I will be nearby watching to make sure that no brave makes sexual advances on her."

"Ha, that would be Roaring Cloud! He is a horny snake, that one! He has already bedded at least a dozen girls in this village. Then there is Little Crow's son, Snowy Owl, who wants her; but she does not want him, and everybody knows that. Well then, you can set up your teepee behind mine. Follow me there and I will show you where to put your teepee."

John and Robert made quick work of their teepee. Then Robert found firewood and John went out to hunt, coming back with a prairie chicken for their dinner. Later that evening, after the sun had set, Little Fox came over to their campfire to sit with Robert.

"My work is done for the day. Come morning, I will be working with the other women and girls preparing the food and packing the supplies the Santee hunters will bring with them. Then tomorrow evening, the men will hold the Buffalo Dance."

"What is the Buffalo Dance?" asked Robert.

His grandfather responded, "Well, let me try to explain its origins to you. As the legend goes, when buffalo first appeared on the earth, they were unfriendly to the Sioux. Like other animals, the Sioux expected them to offer themselves up to the human beings for food, clothing, and tools; but the buffalo did not want this."

"The chief always provided his daughter the best of clothing and the warmest of animal hides to protect her in winter, but it came to pass that the buffalo moved away from the tribe and the people were going to go hungry for lack of meat and suffer the cold for lack of warm buffalo hides."

"One day the chief's daughter traveled alone to the buffalo herd and sang to them that she would marry the buffalo prince if they would provide the wedding feast. In response, a great buffalo bull appeared and announced that he was claiming her as his bride. She went willingly with the buffalo bull and in exchange, her tribe was fed."

"But the chief was not happy with this arrangement and went searching for his daughter. When the buffalo herd realized why he was in their midst, they trampled him to death. The princess was greatly upset but then recalled a reviving song her grandmother had taught her. She sang this song over her dead father, and he returned to life."

"The buffalo were astonished at the chief's return to the living and began to dance as she continued to sing the song. Then the buffalo made a covenant with the princess -- if she would sing the song each time the human beings came to hunt the buffalo, then they would give themselves willingly to the hunters. The souls of the killed buffalo would return in the form of new calves."

"And so today, the Sioux tribes re-enact this legend in their dance before they go out to hunt buffalo."

"Grandfather, I am happy that we are Christians!"

"As am I, Robert, as am I!"

Little Fox just smiled at Robert and leaned into him to cuddle in the warmth of the fire.

🦀🦀🦀

The next day, the first thing in the morning the buffalo hunters and their entourage began their trek. They were traveling west to Dakota Territory where the Santee scouts had spotted a large herd of buffalo. This would be a 150-mile trek and take five days if the weather was favorable. Little Crow announced that they might find some competition from the Pawnee tribe which claimed ownership of these hunting grounds, but he was not worried.

Little Fox usually rode in one of the wagons the Santee brought for hauling buffalo carcasses to be processed by the women. They would be used on the return trip to haul the meat and hides. In the evenings she would do all the chores her mistress told her to do then she would find Robert and his grandfather and sit with them at their campfire.

One evening she was intercepted by Snowy Owl who grabbed her roughly by the arm. Little Fox tried to shake him off and break away from him, but he was too strong.

"What do you see in that half-breed? I am a superior warrior, and I am going to be the village chief someday, you'll see. Kiss me now and experience how a full-blood Santee loves his woman!"

"No, I won't, not ever!" and she kicked him in the groin.

Gasping and sputtering with anger, Snowy Owl attempted to slap her, but she ducked. "Snowy Owl, you have never been kind to me, not once in all these years! How can you expect me or any other girl to love you? Your family has treated me like a slave, not as a daughter. That is not the Santee way. And you just expect to be given everything you want, like you are entitled to it. Well, that might work for many things, but it won't work for me!"

"Just you wait, someday you will be my squaw!" Snowy Owl croaked out to her shoulder as she stepped quickly away. And he resolved then that he would make this promise come true, no matter what it takes.

ᏕᏕᏕ

After five days on the trail, the hunting party came to the area where Arlington, South Dakota now stands. There are several lakes in the region and much green grass which would attract buffalo. Scouts who had been sent ahead came back with news of a large herd found there, but they also witnessed Pawnee Skidi hunters on the south side of the herd.

Hearing this report, Little Crow said he was not worried, "So long as they stay on the south side of the herd and we stay on the east side, there should not be trouble between us."

The Sioux hunting party then traveled to where the big herd was grazing and set up camp near a grove of trees that skirted a lake. By this time, it was close to sunset and the Santee made their evening meals, ate, and then settled in for the night. John Other Day, Robert, and Little Fox sat by their campfire talking about the next day. Little Crow was walking through the camp taking stock of his hunters. As he approached John Other Day's campfire he said,

"Remember John Other Day, no guns when we hunt the buffalo. We don't want to startle the herd and have them stampede away. Use only your bow with arrows, or lance, if you have one. We will hunt in the tradition of our ancestors."

"We will follow your rules, Chief Little Crow!"

"And Little Fox, you will stay here with the women and help them butcher the carcasses."

"Yes, Chief Little Crow. The older women trained me, and I know what I must do. I am ready!"

When the chief left them, John Other Day reminded Robert that piercing a buffalo's lungs through either side of its ribs, caused its two lungs to deflate like a single balloon. Robert would be using his bow and arrows, but John would use his lance.

⤳⤳⤳

At first light the next morning the hunters rode through the large grove of trees until they came to some open ground where the buffalo came to drink from the lake. Armed with 8-foot lances and bows with arrows, the hunters ran their horses into the herd and chose a buffalo to run alongside and stab the animal with their lances or shoot it with arrows until it fell. This process could take several minutes. The buffalo could not survive this trauma.

John Other Day rode his black stallion and Robert rode a brown and white paint horse lent by his friend Silver Wolf, who also was participating in this hunt. With a burst of speed that surprised Robert, John Other Day spurred his black stallion swiftly into the herd and then galloped in parallel to a bull that was fleeing the onslaught. Multiple times he jabbed the bull's side with his lance until the poor beast's lungs were pierced through and the bull snorted his last breath and collapsed in a heap. This process took several minutes.

Up to this point, Robert had been holding back, observing how this drama was played out. Then he decided to plunge into the hunt on his swift painted horse. The horse knew what to do even if Robert was uncertain because he had been used in buffalo hunts before. Robert's steed quickly caught up with a sizable cow, and Robert readied his bow and arrow. This was the first time Robert had tried to shoot while bouncing on a galloping stallion. His first two arrows missed the mark completely, flying over the back of the fleeing cow. His third shot struck the poor creature in the hindquarters, which slowed her down some, but she kept going out of fear. Then figuring he should lead his target some, his fourth arrow struck the animal's side where he thought her lung would be. The snorting dark brown pincushion kept running but was slowing. Robert aimed his fifth arrow closer to the cow's front end and that proved to be the fatal strike. The beast collapsed and did not get up.

Robert looked across the field and saw that Silver Wolf had killed his quarry as well. But wait – he appeared to be in a dispute with Snowy Owl who also had shot at this particular animal from the other side. Snowy Owl claimed his shot was the fatal one, and that he should get the kill. Silver Wolf was saying he would be willing to share the meat with Snowy Owl, but Snowy Owl was adamant – the kill was his alone. Silver Wolf just threw up his arms and found another target.

By afternoon, the Santee hunting party had killed so many buffalo that Little Crow was concerned that they would not have enough wagons to carry the meat and hides back to the village. John Other Day, Robert, and four other hunters including Little Crow and Snowy Owl volunteered to ride back to the camp and fetch the wagons and the women who would butcher the carcasses and process the hides. The remainder of the hunters would stand guard over the carcasses and protect them from the Pawnee if necessary.

As they approached the hunting camp, they noticed that a couple of the wagons had been set on fire as well as three of the tepees. Seeing this, the six Santee hunters urged their horses into a gallop until they entered the camp area. A Santee woman, apparently the oldest of the women with her gray hair, held up her hand to speak to the chief. "Chief Little Crow, we were attacked by a Pawnee raiding party. I could tell by the tongue they spoke. They burned these wagons and tepees, but the only thing they took was a person, the Ojibwa girl, Little Fox. And Chief, these were the renegade Skidi band of the Pawnee Nation. I have seen these people before."

John Other Day was startled when he heard this, and asked, "Which way did the band go?" There was urgency in his voice.

The women all pointed south. John nodded his thanks and caught Robert's eye, "Robert, we must go now while their trail is still fresh. You have your weapons, right?"

"Yes, Grandfather, both my bow and my Colt. But are you taking your lance?"

"No, I will need both hands to shoot my rifle, if it comes to that!"

Snowy Owl said "Wait, I will go with you!" as John and Robert turned to ride away.

But Little Crow said, "No, you will stay here. They took only a slave girl. It is not worth risking your life for her."

"Father, I want this girl for my wife!"

"Son, don't be a fool! The chief's son will not marry an Ojibwa slave girl. These two fools who are chasing after her will only lose their lives. We are in Pawnee territory now, and her would-be rescuers might find her, but she will be held in a village defended by a large number of Pawnee warriors."

With barely suppressed anger, Snowy Owl submitted to this father and rode his horse to where she would be tied up for the night.

CHAPTER NINE

Rescue from the Skidi

The Pawnee Skidi raiding party rode south for six hours at a fast rate and then made camp. Little Fox was bound and gagged and rode with an older warrior who held her in front of him on the horse. He said into her ear in accented Sioux, "Do not be afraid, young daughter. You will be treated like a princess -- you'll see!" But Little Fox was afraid and quite worried.

When the party camped, Little Fox was fed pemmican and nuts, the same food as the warriors. But they did not let her out of their sight, even when she had to urinate, much to her embarrassment. The warriors kept her hands tied behind her back and her ankles bound together even as they turned in for the night sleeping under the stars.

☾☾☾☾

Some days before Little Fox was captured, there was an unlikely meeting of two men from two vastly different cultures. Blue Feather Chouteau, the progeny of an Osage Indian mother and a French St. Louisan father, was a scout for the U.S. Army. He had been sent on a reconnaissance mission to watch the Skidi band of the Pawnee nation, who were rumored to be reverting to a primitive human sacrifice ritual that they had promised to terminate decades earlier. Blue Feather's mission was to collect intelligence on the Skidi and return to Fort Snelling (near St. Paul) where Colonel Sibley would decide what action to take.

Blue Feather was a skilled warrior as well as a scout with excellent tracking skills. He spoke several Indian languages including the various Sioux dialects, Pawnee, and Ojibwa. Blue Feather had a foot in two cultures. His father, a trapper in Missouri, was killed by a mountain lion when Blue Feather was just 10 years old. Not being fully accepted in White society, his mother moved them back to the Osage tribe. But his mother wanted her son to get a white man's education, so she enrolled him at the Indian mission school in Florissant Missouri run by the Jesuit fathers. He excelled in his studies, and he was encouraged to enroll at St. Louis College which was run by the Jesuits. His father's family, the Chouteaus of Saint Louis, insisted on paying for his education. Blue Feather graduated from St. Louis College in 1843.

The other unlikely member of this pair was Yung Wing. Trained in the martial arts (e.g., Kung Fu) by the Shaolin monks in Hong Kong, Yung Wing, then 18 years of age, was one of 24,000 young Chinese men who emigrated to San Francisco for the California gold rush in 1848.

The two men met as they were traveling in opposite directions; Blue Feather riding west in search of the Skidi, Yung Wing riding east in search of adventure and escape from Tong enemies in San Francisco. Given the flat expanse of the prairie with no hills and the low grass, the two men could see each other approaching a common point even at one mile of separation.

The two men met face to face and halted their horses. Blue Feather noticed that the man facing him was Asian, most likely Chinese, given the substantial migration in the past decade. He was not wearing a gun or carrying a rifle but had a bow with a quiver of arrows and a sword. Yung Wing noticed that the man opposite him was probably an Indian, but his facial structure was almost Caucasian. He was wearing buckskins as did most Plains Indians and had a holstered six-gun and a Burnside carbine, a rifle designed for close contact combat. Its range was only 600 feet. Of course, Yung Wing did not know all the specifics of the weapon; he just knew that cavalry soldiers carried this weapon.

The two men silently examined each other for about ten seconds and then since neither man appeared to have evil intent, they introduced themselves almost simultaneously. "My name is Yung Wing, from California."

"And my name is Blue Feather, from Fort Snelling, Minnesota Territory. What is a fellow like you riding this range all alone?"

"I have escaped from San Francisco where I had angered some members of the Tong. Now I travel to explore this great nation."

"Well, there is plenty to see. But it's not all peaceful, with more white settlers arriving by wagon train every day. The Indian tribes see their traditional hunting grounds being diminished by settlers establishing farms wherever they stop."

"Why are you traveling alone, may I ask?"

"I am a U.S. Army scout searching for a band of Indians called the Skidi of the Pawnee Nation. Rumor is that the Skidi are reviving the Morning Star ritual which involves the sacrifice of a young maiden. The Pawnee had decided a couple of decades ago to abandon this practice when they became friendly with the U.S. Army. The Army wants to put an end to this practice if indeed the Skidi have returned to it. Have you seen any signs of an Indian village on your recent travels?"

"Yes, some miles back. I steered clear of them but stopped to observe them through my field glasses. I drew this picture as a record of my experiences," he said, handing a notebook to Blue Feather, who then examined it carefully. "This could be the Skidi! This platform set up in the center of the camp is where the ritual sacrifice would be performed. With this platform set up, the Skidi may have already captured a young girl for the sacrifice. I must go to this camp pronto!"

Yung Wing said, "Wait, I will go with you and help you rescue this girl! I am skilled in the martial arts, trained by the Shaolin monks. Follow me and I will show you the way to their camp."

Blue Feather didn't know what a Shaolin monk was but assumed that they weren't anything like the Jesuit priests who taught him at the mission school or later at St. Louis College.

Without another word, the men galloped off in the direction of the Skidi camp.

It was close to dusk when Blue Feather and Yung Wing approached the Skidi camp. Blue Feather turned to Yung Wing and said, "Let's keep out of sight by riding over to that grove of trees to the left. Then while we observe the camp, we will plan how to rescue the girl."

"Blue Feather, I just saw the flames of a small campfire to the left deep in the trees. I suggest we find out who made this fire as our next step."

"Yes, that is a good idea. Perhaps someone else is distressed about the goings-on in this Skidi camp, and we might want to team up with them."

The men rode into the grove of trees and dismounted, then walked to the campfire leading their horses. A man's voice called out in the Sioux language, "Who approaches our campfire?"

Blue Feather answered in Sioux, "I am Blue Feather, a scout from Fort Snelling; and my companion is Yung Wing, from China."

John Other Day turned to Robert and translated for him. "The man says he is an army scout, and he has a Chinese companion."

"Thanks, Grandfather. I thought that was what he said, but my Sioux is not all that good!"

"Please enter our camp and share our food and coffee."

Blue Feather and Yung Wing tied their horses to a tree close to the steeds of John and Robert.

John Other Day spoke in English, "You two make an unlikely pair. Where are you going?"

"I am on a reconnaissance mission for the Army. My commander wants to know what the Skidi band of the Pawnee nation is up to. He heard that they are reviving a ritual involving human sacrifice that they allegedly had quit doing some decades ago."

"It is good that you found us! My grandson, Robert, and I are hoping to rescue a young girl, Little Fox, who was stolen from a Santee buffalo camp by the Skidi. She is loved in our family, and if she is not rescued, she will be the victim of their sacrifice."

"When was the girl stolen from the Santee camp?"

"It was yesterday afternoon. As soon as we heard of her capture, we began tracking them. We found their camp here. It must be the right camp because the platform they constructed in the center of the camp looks like it will be used in the sacrifice."

"Then we have some time. Are you familiar with the Morning Star Ceremony, John?"

"Yes, once Little Fox has been dedicated to the Morning Star, which has already taken place, she will be treated with respect and kindness. The Skidi will not tell her why she has been captured and why she is receiving special treatment. On the morning of the fifth day, she will be led out to the platform and tied to the scaffold. There she will be killed by warriors shooting arrows at her."

Young Wing said, "This is barbaric! We must rescue the girl, tonight, if possible after the villagers retire to their teepees to sleep."

"There will be at least one warrior guarding the entrance to the teepee where they are keeping Little Fox," said Blue Feather.

"And where will that teepee be?" asked Robert.

"It will be set up right in front of the platform, no more than forty feet away," said Blue Feather.

John Other Day had already formulated a plan, "Here is how we can stage the rescue. Yung Wing, you should go to the rope corral and drive out the Skidis' ponies so their warriors cannot chase after us. Blue Feather, perhaps you can distract attention to the opposite end of the village by setting some teepees on fire and then shouting "Fire" in Pawnee. You speak Pawnee, do you not? I will remove the warriors standing guard over the teepee holding Little Fox; and Robert, you will retrieve Little Fox from her captivity. She will recognize you right away. You will need to bring your Bowie knife to cut her bindings if necessary, and a blanket."

"Any questions? If you have any suggestions speak up now. None? Then let's be ready by the third watch to begin the rescue."

Robert found it hard to sleep that night. He was naturally anxious about their rescue plans. He had every confidence in his grandfather, Blue Feather, and even Yung Wing despite his small stature, but he worried about his own courage and fighting skill. He thought *I must not fail!*

Then he tried to pray and Psalm 21 occurred to him, "The Lord is my light and my salvation; Whom shall I fear? The Lord is the strength of my life; Of whom shall I be afraid?" Then he fell into a deep restful sleep.

The third watch came around 3:00 in the morning. John Other Day awakened everyone, and all saddled their horses. There was a full moon which provided enough light to see where they were going. Then silently and slowly they rode to their appointed places for the rescue attempt. Yung Wing went to the rope enclosure holding the Skidi horses. Blue Feather found his position at the opposite corner of the camp and lit one of two torches he had made. And crouching a hundred feet from the teepee holding Little Fox were John Other Day and Robert. They noticed that there were two guards, perhaps one was relieving the other. John Other Day said to Robert, "I regret that I have no choice but to kill them both. If one gets away to alarm the others, not one of us will get out alive."

"I understand, Grandfather," Robert said looking resigned to the fact.

John raised his bow took aim and killed one guard. As he fell into the arms of the second guard John had already released his second arrow, and the two dead guards fell together in a clump. At that moment Yung Wing cut down the rope corral and ran to the back of the horses and slapped two horses on the butt with the flat of his sword, causing them to whinny and rush forward. As if they were a flock of birds, the horses ran out of their enclosure. Then Yung Wing readied his bow to cut down any warrior running his way.

Seeing the horses flee, Blue Feather quickly set fire to the back of two teepees, and as the flames climbed up the teepees he yelled out "Fire" in Pawnee.

John turned to his grandson and said, "Go get her now!" Robert ran toward the teepee keeping low to the ground.

Reaching the teepee undetected, he entered and Little Fox woke up with a start.

"Who's there? I'll scream!"

"Shh, Little Fox! It's Robert! I'm here to rescue you," and he cut her bindings with his Bowie knife.

Little Fox jumped into his arms and hugged Robert. Robert hugged her back and then realized he was touching bare skin.

"Oh, my goodness! I forgot that they took my clothes -- I'm naked!

Robert stammered a bit saying, "Maybe that's why Grandfather told me to bring this blanket!" Robert draped the blanket over her body trying to avert his eyes, but in the moonlight, he could see that her right half was painted red and her left half black.

Just then a medicine man burst into the teepee and just as he raised his tomahawk and started to call out, Robert reflexively stabbed him in the throat, silencing him. The man fell to the floor, grasping his throat as he bled out.

"Oh my God! I killed a man!"

Little Fox kept her head and said, "Robert, you had no choice! Now we must escape before we are discovered!"

Shaking off his shock at killing a man, Robert led Little Fox to where his horse waited, its reins held by a large rock. No sooner had they mounted than Blue Feather and John Other Day rode up. However, Yung Wing could not yet flee because he was fighting off multiple braves who had run to the now empty rope corral. Blue Feather and John marveled at how he could fight, slashing some attackers with his sword and kicking others senseless. They decided to help him by shooting arrows at oncoming attackers. Then one brave called out

"Get away from him! He is a yellow *Waka Sica* (Devil, wah-kahn shee-chah)." Then the braves quickly withdrew, not even pausing to help their fallen brethren. With their withdrawal, Yung Wing mounted his horse and joined the others.

Little Fox and her rescuers rode through the night aided by the full moon. Blue Feather and Yung Wing had decided to ride with the others as further protection should they be intercepted by angry Skidi. At dawn, they rested and watered their horses at a stream. Their destination was the Perrault farm, where Grandmother Roseanne waited with Makawee and Henri. John Other Day decided not to bother with stopping at Little Crow's hunting camp. John felt that Little Crow had relinquished his claim to Little Fox when he gave her up as lost to the Skidi. He had his two buffalo as agreed on, but he would not get Black Lightning.

☞☞☞

CHAPTER TEN

Homecoming

Upon the men's arrival at the Perrault farm, Roseanne and Makawee ran out of the house followed by Henri. Their joy mixed with confusion when they noticed Little Fox was wearing nothing but a blanket, and that her body (what they could see of it) was painted black and red.

"What on earth happened to Little Fox? asked Roseanne. Then realization dawned on her,

"Omigosh, you were attacked by the Skidi, and they stole Little Fox!"

"Yes, that is right. I will tell you the whole story later. But thank God we met these two new friends, Blue Feather and Yung Wing who helped us rescue Little Fox!"

Little Fox began to cry and ran to the arms of Roseanne. "Come now, daughter and we will wash this paint off you. Henri, get some warm water for a bath; and Makawee, please get some clean clothes for Little Fox."

Henri jogged over to the washhouse he had built, which included its own well pump and fireplace for heating water. The outhouse was separate and downhill from the washhouse.

Henri noticed a troubled look on Robert's face and gently pulled him aside, "Robert, is something bothering you?"

"Pa, I killed a man...I acted reflexively and stabbed him with my Bowie knife. If I had time to think about it, I might have just knocked him out. But he came barging into the teepee where

Little Fox was being held captive and was about to scream for help! If help came, then we might not have escaped."

Henri sighed and stared down at his shoes for a second, then he looked up at Robert with a mournful expression. "Robert, when I was younger than you, just twelve, the Black Hawk war was going on. At the time, my father had a farm in Illinois. One day while my father was in town getting supplies, a band of Sac Indians attacked our farm. I was alone with my mother, and it was my duty to protect her. I had my musket at the door and a single-shot pistol near the front window. I fired the musket at one brave as he ran toward the door, killing him instantly. Then I ran to the window and shot a second brave approaching the door. Meanwhile, my mother had reloaded the musket by the door, and I fired a third time, winging a brave on the shoulder. The rest of the band must have thought there were multiple shooters in the house and decided it wasn't worth the risk. So that day I killed two Sac braves. I will always regret these deaths, but I had to defend my mother."

"So, Pa, how did you learn to live with these killings? I can't get what I did out of my mind!"

"Well, Son eventually I gained some perspective on what I had done, helped by the assurances I received from friendly adults. Later that day, militiamen arrived at the farm. They were tracking the band of Sac Indians who attacked us. I told their officer, a young captain named Lincoln, what had happened. He told me that I had shown courage and that I had done the right thing. Son, the best I can do for you is to say the same -- what Captain Lincoln said to me applies to you as well."

Blue Feather stayed overnight at the Perrault farm, becoming fast friends with John Other Day; but then he had to return to Fort Snelling to make his report to Colonel Sibley. Yung Wing stayed with the Perrault family for a week, fascinated with Henri's workshop, as he was something of a gunsmith and tinker himself.

Impressed by Henri's redesign of the repeating air gun, Yung Wing drew up plans for a repeating crossbow, a weapon that had seen use in China for centuries.

"Henri, I have a design I want to show you!"

"Another type of repeating rifle?"

"No, but something that serves the same function but with a completely different mechanism. This weapon has been used in China for 1,600 years. It is a repeating crossbow! The repeating crossbow makes it possible to string the bow, place the bolt, and shoot using the motion of just one hand, thus enabling a much faster launch rate than a normal crossbow; in fact, about one bolt every two seconds. This is a top-mounted magazine that holds a number of bolts that are fed to the crossbow through gravity. This rectangular lever is moved forward and backward to draw the string and launch the bolt. Chinese peasants used a small version of this kind of weapon against marauders attacking their villages and homes. A larger version was mounted on the gunwales of fighting ships. Depending on the size of the bow, the repeating crossbow has an effective range of about ninety yards and a maximum range of almost two hundred yards."

"We need to build one of these repeating crossbows!"

"Why? You must realize it is a defensive weapon. It would be useful in repelling invaders, but not much more."

"Yung Wing, the time will come, I'm afraid when farmers like me will have to defend their homes and families from Santee Indians on the warpath."

"But isn't John Other Day a Santee Indian?"

"Yes, but there is a substantial number within the Santee nation who want to chase White settlers out of Minnesota, and those who don't flee will be killed. If there is a crop failure and the game continues to migrate from this area, the Santee will go hungry and become desperate for food. Then they will attack."

Yung Wing stared at Henri for a couple of seconds then said, "Well, then let's build one!"

The repeating crossbow took four weeks to build from wood and metal. This included some tests and adjustments, but no major modifications. Then Henri shared his ideas on how the weapon might be deployed.

"Yung Wing, you noticed the balcony that covers the porch of our house? Well, I'm thinking that I could mount one or two of these repeating crossbows on the balcony rails."

"You are turning your home into a fortress! Do you expect this much trouble from the Santee?"

"With a nod and a sigh, Henri said, "Yes, in fact, I do."

Henri showed Yung Wing his drawings that would allow the weapon to pivot horizontally and vertically, with cogwheel and pawl mechanisms that would secure its position. Then over a matter of days, they built the mechanism, mounted the weapon on the balcony rails, and put it to the test. It worked very well from the start.

☙☙☙

CHAPTER ELEVEN

Yung Wing continued his stay with the Perrault family, sleeping on a cot in the workshop. One day Robert approached him with a request, "Can you teach me to fight the way you do?"

"Robert, I can teach you how to defend yourself, but not so that you would attack others!"

"That's what I am interested in learning, how to defend myself in case I am attacked."

"Then we will start our lessons tomorrow morning after your chores."

標標標標

"The Shaolin monks teach Kung Fu as a part of a whole philosophy of being. You must tend to both mind and body when you begin to learn Kung Fu. The physical practice affects your mental growth and vice versa. So today we will start by learning the basic stances and moves. Tomorrow we will continue with various kinds of kicks, and then, punches and blocks over the course of weeks."

Robert practiced his lessons each day as winter approached. And one day he found that he was forced to use his new skills. He was out bow-hunting in the woods when he heard derisive laughter and boys shouting in German, *"Lass uns in Ruhe. Wir haben dir nichts angetan!*" (Leave us alone. We did not do anything to you.)

He jogged deeper in the woods to where he thought the commotion was and saw two young Indian braves abusing Karl and Wilhelm Bauer, his neighbors from the farm next to the Perrault farm. Karl was fourteen and Wilhelm was just twelve. In a clearing in the woods, the Santees abusing them were Roaring Cloud who was twenty years of age, and Snowy Owl, now seventeen.

The Santee braves had their backs were to him as he emerged from the woods. "Stop that! Leave those boys alone."

"Well, look who it is! No six-guns with you today, half breed?" said Roaring Cloud, who then started to bring down his tomahawk at Robert. Robert blocked the downward swing of the weapon with his forearm and kicked his assailant in the gut causing him to fall hard backward. As he was lying there winded, Robert grabbed his tomahawk and threw it far away.

"Snowy Owl, you let him take my tomahawk?! Let me have yours!"

To his credit, Snowy Owl said, "No, you picked this fight against an unarmed boy, now you must face him on equal terms."

Robert was taller (five feet ten inches) and heavier by fifteen pounds than his opponent; and he was strong, farm-strong from doing a lot of physical labor. He was also flexible from his practice of kung fu.

Roaring Cloud spat and scrambled to his feet. "Why are you standing and moving like that? Are you going to dance?" Then he lunged at Robert, who dodged him, and then tripped him. Roaring Cloud ate some dirt on that fall and now his nose was bleeding.

Roaring Cloud growled and scrambled unsteadily to his feet. Then he charged Robert again swinging his fist wildly at Robert's face. Deflecting the blow, Robert landed two quick blows, one to the stomach and a second to his opponent's jaw. As he reeled backward, Robert landed a kick to his face. Roaring Cloud fell hard on his back, defeated.

"Get out of here before he recovers!" Snowy Owl hissed, knowing that Roaring Cloud would be mad enough to kill Robert and the Bauer brothers.

"Come on, let's go!" said Robert motioning the boys in the direction of their farm.

Robert ran with the Bauer boys to their farm which was on the way to the Perrault farm. When they arrived there, Herr Josef Bauer greeted them as they walked into the household mudroom.

"Well, hello Herr Robert! I did not expect to see you *mit mein Sohne!*"

The younger Bauer boy blurted out, "*Robert hat einen Inder für uns bekämpft!*" (Robert fought an Indian for us.)

"*Was ist das? Stimmt das, dass Sie von einem Inder angegriffen wurden?*

Oh, excuse me, let me say this in English! What is this? Is this true that you were attacked by an Indian?"

"*Ja, Vater, wir wurden von einem Inder angegriffen und Robert kam uns zu Hilfe.*" (Yes, Father, we were attacked by an Indian and Robert came to our aid.)

"Robert, thank you for protecting my boys. We belong to the German Baptist Brethren church, and we do not engage in fighting. We turn the other cheek. But now I am wondering if this is a practical way to live in this country with wild savages."

"Herr Bauer, I would not call them savages, at least not the majority of them. But some do not behave in a civilized manner, and they do not have the same sense of right and wrong as we have based on the Christian faith."

The next day the Bauer family led by Josef and his wife, Elfriede, visited the Perrault farm. They brought a ham, smoked in their own smokehouse, and a large jar of apple butter.

"Henri and Makawee, did your son Robert tell you how he saved our sons from an Indian attack? No? Well, he bravely fought a young warrior who might have seriously hurt our boys; and we are so grateful! These gifts are just a small token of our gratitude."

Henri and Makawee welcomed the Bauers into their home and the two families had a pleasant visit. From that day forward a deep friendship grew between the two families. Robert finally had won friends among the white settlers; and when the word spread of his fight with Roaring Cloud, he found acceptance and even respect and admiration in New Ulm. Unfortunately, the fight also soured if not spoiled his relationship with the Santee. But not with Silver Wolf, who rode to the Perrault farm one day to warn Robert to not try to visit Little Crow's village anymore. He rode one horse and towed a second, the painted horse he had lent Robert for the buffalo hunt.

"Hey, welcome Silver Wolf! What brings you to our farm?"

"Hi, Robert! Well, it's not good news, I'm afraid. I came to warn you about the talk in the village these days. Roaring Cloud has been telling everyone who will listen that you used sorcery against him when you defeated him in the fight you two had."

"Sorcery? No, it was Kung Fu that I used. It is a Chinese martial art that our friend Yung Wing taught me."

"Chinese? Oh, you mean those yellow-skinned foreigners I've heard about."

"There are many types of people in the world today, Silver Wolf, and this land that the Indians once solely had to themselves now attracts people from all around the world."

"Little Crow and other chiefs feel like the Santee and other nations like the Ojibwa, Pawnee, and Osage will be crowded out and we will lose our traditional way of life."

"I'm sorry to say that I think it is bound to happen. Say, why did you bring the painted horse with you?"

"Well, Robert, I came here to warn you not to try to visit the village anymore, at least not until things calm down. This could be our last meeting for quite a while. And I want to give this painted horse to you as a token of our friendship. I'll never forget you!"

Robert was dumbfounded at first but graciously accepted the gift. "I will take good care of him, don't you worry! But I don't have anything for you!"

"Well, there is something you can do for me -- could you tell me about your God and his Son Jesus?"

Robert smiled broadly and responded, "I would be very happy to! Let's sit down and I'll tell you everything I know and read to you God's word recorded in the Bible."

When he finished, he told Silver Wolf that he could learn more from John Other Day and Roseanne, his grandparents, whose farm was close to the Santee village. But Silver Wolf wanted to commit his life without delay, "Is there not a prayer or ritual we can do so that I might become a disciple of Jesus, and have his protection?" And so, Robert said with him a prayer of salvation, where he dedicated his life to Jesus.

Thus, the young men parted with an even deeper friendship, reminiscent of David and Jonathan in the Bible.

෯෯෯

CHAPTER TWELVE

A Brief Calm Before the Storm

Little Fox went to live with John and Roseanne and became their daughter. This was the happiest time in her life besides the early years with her natural parents. John was very protective of her, so much so that he rode with her when she wanted to visit the Perrault family at their farm or go to New Ulm for shopping. Robert visited the Other Days three or four times a week, even during winter through the heavy Minnesota snow, riding his brown and white paint horse.

Robert became good friends with the Bauer brothers, Karl and Wilhelm. He helped them learn English and occasionally would ride into New Ulm with them where he was treated as a local hero of sorts because he had protected the Bauer brothers from belligerent Indians.

Robert and Little Fox discussed marriage. They were sure of their love but felt that they were too young at seventeen to get married. Besides, Robert was still unsure of what occupation to follow even though he was a competent farmer. Henri had taken Robert on as a gunsmith apprentice, so that occupation was still an option.

Yung Wing decided to stay on at the Perrault farm and Henri had built an addition to the workshop where Yung Wing and Henri worked side-by-side. This included space for an actual bedroom for Yung Wing. Henri also decided to expand his business and added locksmith to his skills and services offered. The business was steady.

Minnesota had been admitted to the union in 1858 and hardly two years had passed when talk of southern states seceding from the union had begun. Henri thought that this would likely mean civil war and it bothered him that Robert would be the prime age for enlistment as a Union soldier. In the meantime, there was plenty to be concerned about close to home. Wild game had become even more scarce, and the buffalo herds had moved further away due to encroaching farmland. Then, making matters worse, there was a crop failure in 1861, and many Santee nearly starved during the winter of 1861-1862.

ॐॐॐ

CHAPTER THIRTEEN

The Sioux Uprising Begins

In the spring of 1861, several southern states seceded from the union and the civil war began. After the bombardment of Fort Sumter and its surrender, President Lincoln called for the formation of a 75,000-man militia that would serve for ninety days. Nearly all the northern states answered the call, except for the border states of Missouri, Kentucky, Maryland, and Delaware; but each of these states eventually decided to side with the Union. Virginia was also initially considered a border state but then the state legislature voted for secession. In response, fifty counties broke away from the rest of Virginia to form a new state called West Virginia which was loyal to the union.

In Minnesota patriotism ran high and regiments formed quickly. But Robert did not enlist because he was especially needed on the farm after his father, Henri, was knocked down and nearly trampled by a bull that had broken loose from a neighbor's farm. He was seriously injured but the prognosis was good. Nonetheless, his recovery would take months.

Responsibilities for the farm fell on Robert, and Yung Wing had to assume all the work for their gunsmith and locksmith business. They managed, but it was hard to be down a person. In the meantime, Makawee did her best to nurse Henri back to health following the doctor's orders but also making use of some Indian remedies to relieve pain.

In 1861 crop failure was widespread in Minnesota, followed by an especially harsh winter. It was followed by more crop failures the next summer. The Santee population was near starvation by August 1862 and the tensions between the white settlers and the Santee Indians were about to boil over.

Santee women came to Chief Little Crow to complain that they didn't have enough food to feed their families. One woman spoke for them all when she said, "Some of the white farmers are sharing their produce with us, if they have any excess, accepting our promise of sharing our game in the future; and John Other Day, who is one of us, is sharing his produce without expecting anything in return. But we are close to starving! You can hear the little children crying, can't you? They are hungry and we have nothing to give them!"

"I have been to the Indian Agency warehouse with my son Snowy Owl. The government men there said that they could not let us buy food on credit even though it is their own government that is late in sending the Santee their annuity payments!"

One of the mothers replied, "Some of the agency storekeepers gave us food earlier this summer; but now this man Andrew Myrick has refused us, saying, 'If they are hungry, let them eat grass.'"

A flicker of rage crossed the face of Chief Little Crow when he heard this. Then he regained his composure and said, "I will call a council of the Sioux chiefs whose bands are affected by this dearth of food. Together we will figure out what we should do. Snowy Owl, choose a courier to send to each of the Santee bands living nearby and send their chiefs a message that I want to hold a council here the day after tomorrow to discuss this problem." Snowy Owl nodded yes and quickly left to choose the messengers.

෬෬෧෧

Four young Santee braves were returning from an unsuccessful hunting trip when one of them discovered some chicken
eggs near a farmhouse.[2] He was stooping to pick them up
when one of his companions said, "Wait, don't steal those eggs
from this white farmer! That will only cause trouble between us
and the white man." The brave with the eggs threw them down
in disgust and said, "You are afraid of the white man. You are
afraid of him even though you are starving!"

Another companion said, "I will show you that I am not
afraid of the white man -- I will go to his house and shoot him
dead. Who is brave enough to come with me?"

The four braves rode on to the farm of Robinson Jones who
was standing in his barnyard with his neighbors Howard Baker
and Veronious Webster.

The brave who was most fluent in English spoke for them,
"Farmer Jones, we hear that you are the best marksmen among
your people in these parts. We want to challenge you in a
friendly shooting contest."

"Well, I would never claim to be the best! My friends here,
Mr. Baker or Mr. Webster, might be just as good or better than
I am with a rifle. We are all veterans of the war with Mexico."

"Then let them join in the competition."

With that, Mr. Jones set up a row of tin cans on the corral
fence, one for each of the four Indians and the three farmers.
The Santee took their shots first, deliberately missing so that
they could reload. Then the three farmers took their turns, each
hitting their targets. They did not bother to reload. Then without provocation, the braves turned their rifles on the farmers
and shot them dead. Hearing the initial shots, Mrs. Jones and
her adopted daughter had come out from the farmhouse, and

they too were killed. Whooping with delight, the braves raided the smokehouse and carried off the hams, bacon, and other pork they found there, escaping on horseback.

The day before the council of Santee chiefs convened, the news broke about the murder of three white farmers, a woman, and a girl by four young warriors from Chief Big Eagle's band. The chiefs Mankato, Wabasha, Big Eagle, and Traveling Hail upon hearing this news agreed among themselves that this would be the time for the Santee to take the offensive and not wait for the U.S. Army to march on their villages; and when the council of chiefs met this is the opinion they shared with Chief Little Crow.

At first Chief Little Crow did not want to go to war saying, "Braves, you are like little children -- you know not what you do. You are full of the white man's devil water; you are like dogs in the hot moon that snap at their own shadows. We are like little herds of buffalo; the great herds are no more. The whites are as many as the locusts. Kill one or ten whites and ten times ten will come to kill you. Count your fingers all day long and the whites with guns will come faster than you can count."

When it looked like Little Crow was not going to declare war on the white settlers, a brash young brave cried out, "Little Crow is a coward!"

In response, Little Crow grabbed the headdress from the offending brave and threw it to the ground, saying, "I am not a coward. I have never backed down from the Ojibwa in our many conflicts. I have taken many scalps -- see them on my lodge pole? But you are foolish! If we go to war against the white man, eventually we will lose; and chances are, we will be pushed off these lands which hold the bones of our ancestors. They will come in swarms like locusts, destroying everything in their paths. No, war would be foolish."

But despite his initial protests and warnings, the other chiefs voted that Little Crow should lead the war against the white settlers. One of the other chiefs said, "This is the time to wage war while the white men are foolishly engaged in a war between the northern and southern tribes of their nation. The nearby forts have only small numbers of soldiers. Not enough to stop us."

Reluctantly Little Crow agreed to be the war chief. Almost immediately Santee braves began forming war parties and fanned out from their villages. The Santee were merciless in their attacks, killing every man they encountered, raping the women, burning fields and homes, and stealing all they could carry. Among the first white men to be killed was Andrew Myrick, who was found dead on his lawn with his mouth stuffed with grass.

Two of the most belligerent braves in the village, Snowy Owl and Roaring Cloud, gathered their friends into one group of about thirty warriors. Immediately these two rivals began to argue over who should be the leader of the raiding party. Snowy Owl was the first to address the group.

"I had a vision where the Great Spirit, Wakan Tanka, appeared to me and told me to rise up against the white men and seek revenge against him for destroying our way of life. We are to ride forth and destroy all of the white man's farms and homes and kill as many as we can, starting with the men and the boys. Then we can do what we please with the women and girls, and take the white man's meat, wheat, and corn so that our people can eat."

"Do not listen to this boy! This is the foolish boy who invited that white boy into our village only to be humiliated by him in archery. I am the more experienced warrior, and I will not hesitate to kill the white man. You need a man like me to lead you, not an inexperienced boy who has not killed before."

"That same white boy humiliated you in hand-to-hand combat, oh great warrior!"

Then the rivals began wrestling while the other young braves looked on in bewilderment. All looked up when Little Crow walked up and reprimanded the young hotheads.

"Stop it you fools! Save your energies for the fight against the white man! Snowy Owl, you will lead a war party of fifteen braves; and you, Roaring Cloud, will lead another war party of fifteen braves. Young men, stand with the leader you want to follow."

The warriors broke into two groups, each group aligning themselves with the leader closer to their own age. Roaring Cloud's friends were about twenty to twenty-two years of age, and Snowy Owl's friends were about sixteen to eighteen. Roaring Cloud set off to avenge himself against John Other Day who had once thrown him to the dirt in his farmyard. But Snowy Owl led his warriors in the direction of the Perrault farm where he expected to find both Robert and Little Fox. Long pent-up grudges were driving him with a blood lust to kill a young man who at one time considered him a friend. With Robert out of the picture, he would capture Little Fox as his squaw. By killing the half-breed and capturing the girl, his life would be set right.

Snowy Owl shouted to his war party, "Get your weapons and mount up. We will take the southern route toward the white village they call New Ulm. As soon as I see fifteen warriors behind me, we will begin our raids."

Silver Wolf, who had become Robert's best friend among the Santee, had listened quietly, but he was definitely against waging war on the white settlers. As he walked away Snowy Owl noticed and called out to him, "Silver Wolf, aren't you going to join us in our glorious war and drive out the white man once and for all?" When Silver Wolf sighed, Snowy Owl continued,

"Well, of course not! You became friends with that half-breed that used to visit us. Have you become a Christian like him? That is a religion for weaklings who believe in a cowardly god who could not even protect himself from his enemies. Bah! I am done with you. You don't belong with us anymore."

Silver Wolf walked away thinking, *God said, 'Thou shalt not kill.' And if I do nothing to warn the white settlers who will be Snowy Owl's victims, then I am enabling their murder! But if I ride like the wind, I can warn the Perrault family of Snowy Owl's plans.* Without further debate, Silver Wolf grabbed his weapons, jumped on his horse, and rode like the wind to the Perrault farm.

☙❧❦❧❦☙

John Other Day could see the smoke of various farms burning in the distance and leaped into action. "Roseanne, we must escape right now, there is no time to waste because the Santee are on the warpath attacking settlers' farms."

"John, would they not leave us alone if they see we are Indians?"

"At this point, they are so crazed with blood they won't even bother to check!"

"Where is Little Fox?"

"She is in the garden harvesting some vegetables."

John ran out the back door and yelled, "Little Fox, bring your baskets and put them in the buckboard! We must leave immediately for Makawee's farm. The Santees are on the warpath destroying and killing everything in their path!"

Little Fox did what she was told to do, then ran into the house to get Roseanne. She found Roseanne in a near panic, not knowing what to take with her. Little Fox said, "Here, Mother

-- let's take the Bible and your money jar. We won't need anything else. Now, let's run."

John ran back into the house to get his rifle and ammunition, and a bow with a quiver of arrows. He had his tomahawk, unused for the past 35 years, on his belt. "Are you ready? We must go now!"

They ran to the buckboard where John had hitched his mules and tethered his prize black stallion, Black Lightning. In the back of the buckboard, he had Little Fox hold the new calf so that the Holstein mother would surely follow.

On their way to the Perrault farm, a solo Santee rider galloped past them, only to halt his horse, and wait for the buckboard wagon to catch up. The rider said, "Are you John Other Day? I am Silver Wolf of the Little Crow band."

"Yes, I am, why do you ask?"

"I am riding to the Perrault farm, where my friend Robert lives, to warn them that a Santee war party of fifteen braves led by Snowy Owl is on their way to destroy their farm and kill everyone there."

"We are on our way there now! I figured I could not defend my family and farm on my own, so we are fleeing to Henri Perrault's farm. He is married to our daughter."

"That was a wise choice because another war party of fifteen braves is headed toward your farm now if they are not already there! I will race ahead to the Perrault farm to help them prepare for the attack!"

"Thank you, son! These are precious minutes, there is no time to spare."

They made the twelve-mile run to the Perrault farm in record time. As they pulled through the gate, they could see Henri on his balcony surveying the burning farm homes and fields in the distance. Henri was much improved but still moved stiffly after his period of recovery from the bull attack. He had mounted a strange-looking contraption on the balcony rail. Later he explained that it was a repeating crossbow.

Henri called down to John Other Day, "Oh, thank God you are here! Robert's friend, Silver Wolf, told us you were on your way." Then calling into the house, "Robert, go help your grandfather move his animals into the barn. Hurry, we have no time to waste!"

Robert ran to the buckboard and lifted down Little Fox. They embraced and kissed and quickly turned to their tasks. Robert lifted down the newborn calf and Little Fox led her and her mother to the animal barn. Robert unhitched the mules and untethered Black Lightning and started to lead them to the barn as well. But John Other Day took the tether for the black stallion from him, "Robert, I will need Black Lightning for what I must do next!"

With a worried expression, Roseanne said, "What are you thinking of doing, John?"

"I must warn the other white farmers to escape. There is no way a farmer armed only with a squirrel gun can defend himself against Santee warriors! I will ride to the northeast and try to lead a group to safety across the river to Fort Ridgely.

"John, if that is what you believe the Lord is leading you to do, then go. We have four men here to defend us."

"There is Henri, Robert, and Yung Wing... who is the fourth man?"

Then as if on cue, Silver Wolf appeared from the back of the house and called up to Henri,

"Henri, all of the shutters are nailed shut now!"

"Young man, Silver Wolf is it? You know that if you stay here and fight against the Santee war party, you will not be able to return home, do you not?"

"John Other Day, not all Santee of fighting age are participating in this war, so perhaps there will be some village to return to. Robert is my friend, and because of his witness, I am a Christian now. And Christians do not kill, rape, or steal like these Santee warriors! I am a disciple of Christ; I stand against this evil."

"Son, you will always have a home with us, on my farm."

"Thank you, sir."

John Other Day kissed his wife and daughters and waved goodbye to everyone as he jumped on his black stallion to help lead settler families to safety at Fort Ridgely.

Just then a wagon carrying the Bauer family wheeled through the gate. Mrs. Bauer, obviously distraught, was crying and sobbing,

"*Unser Zuhause, unser Bauernhof. Alles wird von den Indianern zerstört!*" [Our home, our farm. Everything will be destroyed by the Indians!] Makawee ran up to her and hugged her as she got off the wagon. "You and your family will be safe with us. You did the right thing coming here. We will all have to rebuild after this war. We'll help each other!"

"*Vielen Dank, Frau Perrault. Du bist ein wahrer Freund!*" Then in English after a moment's thought, "Thank you, you are a true friend!"

Mr. Bauer yelled to his boys, "Boys, unhitch the wagon and put the mules in the corral, schnell! Henri, the Indians are just one farm away and after they finish with our farm, they will be here!"

"Listen, everyone, Robert, Yung Wing, and Silver Wolf will be the ground-level defenders. On the balcony, we will have Mr. Bauer on the repeating crossbow, Makawee on the bow, and me with my air rifle. Our goal on the balcony is to take out as many warriors as they first enter the gate. Your goal on the ground level is to take out whoever gets past the first volley of fire. I will join you at that point. Mr. Bauer, you will stay on the second floor. I showed you how to operate the crossbow. You can also detach it and use it as a hand weapon to defend the women and children if needed. We must cut the attackers down before they get to the top of the stairs!

Looking up, Henri noticed that a column of smoke was rising above the Bauer's farm. He shouted, "OK, everyone. Not finding anyone to kill at the Bauer's farm they are headed here. We are going to send them away with their tails between their legs!"

Fifteen riders came galloping to the gate, which Henri had closed and locked. Two warriors dismounted to see if they could destroy the lock. That was enough time for the long-range weapons to release a barrage. Henri's air rifle made practically no more noise than did Makawee's bow. Before they knew what was happening, four warriors were struck down, including the two who had dismounted and chopped open the gate. Henri and Makawee kept up their volley and two more warriors were taken out. The remaining nine warriors rode through the gate, although at a much slower speed.

"Start shooting now, Mr. Bauer," Henri shouted over the Santee war cries. And Mr. Bauer, for a pacifist, fought well, striking down two more warriors with the crossbow. Robert opened fire with his Colt six-gun using his shoulder stock. He killed one warrior and wounded a second in a place where the warrior would have traded for a bullet in the heart. One warrior dismounted and made the mistake of attacking Yung Wing, thinking of him as a strange small yellow man of little significance. As he raised his tomahawk to begin his downswing, Yung Wing's sword relieved him of his weapon and his hand. The warrior staggered back and stared in disbelief at his missing limb, then ran off in search of his steed.

That left four warriors including Snowy Owl. The other three warriors quickly abandoned him, the last to leave. As he approached the gate, he stopped and turned to shout, "This fight isn't over yet -- I will return!"

ᏚᏚᏚ

CHAPTER FOURTEEN

After John Other Day delivered a group of about one hundred refugees to safety at Fort Ridgely, he set out again to see if he could escort more refugees to safety to the north. As he galloped in a northwesterly direction, he could see farmhouses burning in the distance, including his own. From the conditions of the flames and columns of smoke, John inferred that the warriors were working their way north, toward the Upper Sioux Agency. John was determined to evacuate as many white settlers as he could and get them to a brick building in that compound.

By happenstance, John ran into Blue Feather who was reconnoitering the situation for the U.S. Army at Fort Ridgely. Recognizing Blue Feather in the distance by his distinctive palomino pony, John called out, "Blue Feather, it is John Other Day!"

"Good to see you John, but business first! What can you tell me about the uprising so far? I am on a reconnaissance mission for Colonel Sibley. What areas are in danger?"

"All white settlers in the Minnesota River valley are in danger. Some war parties went north, and some went south toward New Ulm. I am riding now to round up as many farmers and their families as I can and take them to a brick building in the Upper Sioux Agency where they can hide and be safe at least for tonight."

"Then I will help you! Then I must return to report to Colonel Sibley by telegraph. He will deploy soldiers from Fort Snelling as well as Fort Ridgely to protect the white farmers."

⁌⁌⁌⁌

Roaring Cloud and his war party joined the stream of other war parties heading back to Little Crow's village. They had not yet held a proper War Dance and would do that now. About three hundred women and girls had been captured. Their husbands and sons had been killed, and many of the women and girls had been raped, and now trudged along wearing just straps of torn clothing. The warriors left them at the village with just a few braves to watch over them and prevent their escape. There was much weeping, and these surviving captives without hope presented such a forlorn sight that many of the Santee women felt pity for them.

The leaders of the war parties met to plan their next steps. Roaring Cloud noticed Snowy Owl's severely diminished war party and said loud enough for all to hear, "It seems that the warriors who chose to follow you chose unwisely! I count only three of the fifteen braves who joined your war party, and no captives. What happened? Did the farmers pelt you with cow and mule dung, or rotten eggs? Or perhaps the farmers told their hogs to attack you? This is a pitiful showing for the son of a chief!"

"We attacked the farm of the half-breed's parents, but they were well-prepared for battle, with strange weapons. The traitor Silver Wolf was there. He must have warned the family of our attack."

"How many men were defending the farm?"

"Besides Silver Wolf, there was the half-breed and his fa-ther, a German farmer, and a strange little yellow man who was deadly with both his bow and his long knife."

"Five men, if you can call them that, fought off fifteen Santee warriors? That is embarrassing!"

"There also was a woman there who was the best archer I've ever seen!"

"What?! The half-breed's mother chased you away?" With that thought, Roaring Cloud rolled on the ground laughing at Snowy Owl, who stomped off.

Little Crow appeared and called the warriors to attention. "Go to your families with the meat you have captured. Prepare your meals and eat. Tomorrow we will go out again before the soldiers arrive here from Fort Ridgely and Fort Snelling. We will go to the German village, New Ulm, and kill all the men and boys there. This must be a concerted effort because the village is large and will be swollen with additional farmers fleeing our wrath. But do not kill the women and children! White men do not kill women and children. If we harm them, we will be call-ing down the wrath of their god, and the soldiers will fight us even more severely."

⚬⚬⚬

Before the day was over, John had escorted about one hun-dred white settlers to Fort Ridgely for safety. Then he headed north rounding up an additional sixty-two white settlers whom he led to the Upper Sioux Agency, where he temporarily hid them in a large brick building. He stood guard over this hiding place overnight. When the Santee did not reappear, John set out to lead the settlers on a ninety-mile journey to Fort Snelling to get them as far from the conflict as possible.

In the meantime, the commander at Fort Ridgely, Captain John Marsh, decided to dispatch some troops to defend New Ulm while keeping a force to defend the fort. He also telegraphed Colonel Sibley at Fort Snelling to advise him of the uprising and that the Santee were likely to gather in numbers to attack the town of New Ulm. In response, the colonel dispatched two companies of regular soldiers with orders to increase their force with militia from nearby towns and Fort Ridgely. At Fort Ridgely, two companies of the 5th Minnesota Volunteer Infantry joined in to defend New Ulm, and Blue Feather rode with them as their scout. In the meantime, the residents built barricades around the town, and those who had firearms prepared for the attack.

It took John Other Day four days to lead the sixty-two refugees to Fort Snelling. When he finally arrived both man and beast were greatly fatigued. John and his black stallion rested overnight, with John camping under the stars near the horse barn. He awoke with the bugler playing Reveille and Colonel Sibley standing over him.

"You must be John Other Day! I am Colonel Sibley, commander at this fort. Blue Feather telegraphed me about your courageous deed in leading these refugees to safety. Now I want to recruit you as a scout to work alongside your friend Blue Feather, to find and track the belligerent Santee. Of course, the Army will pay you for your service."

"I will be pleased to help the Army protect the white settlers."

"Great, then come with me and we'll get a proper breakfast for you."

Then shortly after a quick breakfast, John led two companies of U.S. Army cavalry in the direction of New Ulm. This was a ninety-mile trip, but if they kept their horses at a steady ten-mile-per-hour lope, they could arrive at their destination in just over ten hours. Some of the soldiers would reinforce Fort Ridgely, which might be attacked, and the others rode on to New Ulm to reinforce the troops already there to protect the village from Santee invasion or to engage them if the attack had already started. Colonel Sibley was going to follow at a much slower pace with infantry and artillery.

As Blue Feather and the soldiers from Fort Ridgely approached New Ulm, Blue Feather requested permission to ride on to the Perrault farm to check on his friends. Since he was not strictly a combatant, permission was granted, and Blue Feather galloped the three miles to the farm.

Everyone was happy to see Blue Feather but even before he dismounted, Roseanne and Makawee asked if he knew of John's whereabouts. Blue Feather responded, "I met up with John when he was planning to escort a group of refugees to the Upper Agency headquarters for safety. The last I heard is that John was leading a group of refugees to Fort Snelling. I didn't go with him because I had to report to the commander at Fort Ridgely."

Henri then related what had happened with the attack by a war party of fifteen Santee braves, of which only four or five survived the battle.

"They retrieved their dead that night, which I expected them to do," Roseanne said.

"I was relieved to see the bodies removed as well -- I didn't want our farm to become a burial place for our enemies," said Makawee.

"Well then, it's good that I buried the hand I severed in the woods off your property," said Yung Wing.

Roseanne just looked up to heaven and said a silent prayer.

"Just before Snowy Owl galloped out of here, he said he would return. I'm pretty sure that he won't be alone," said Robert.

"Snowy Owl could return with twice as many braves as last time," said Blue Feather.

"I can't believe that Snowy Owl was once my friend! Why is he so bent on attacking us?"

Little Fox hugged Robert and said, "It is because he wants me! He intends to kill you and capture me thinking that he can force me to be his squaw!"

"That will never happen!" exclaimed Robert as he hugged her.

"No, we'll never let that happen!" Roseanne said emphatically, looking to Henri and Makawee, who said in unison, "Of course not."

Mr. Bauer joined their conversation asking, "Would we be safer in New Ulm?"

Henri responded, "Possibly, yes. But I want to protect this home from the destruction your home suffered, and in transit, we might be attacked by a war party. To prevent the destruction of this farm, we must remain here. Listen, I have something to show you all, and then I need help to put them in place." And then with a hand gesture, Henri led the men to the back of the barn where he had stored a large pile of *chevaux de frise*. "I have been making these for a few years now. We have enough to encircle the house."

"What are these things?" asked Blue Feather.

"They are a defensive barrier called *chevaux de frise*.

Mr. Bauer then interjected "Of course, I recognize these now. The name means Frisian horses. Friesland is a region partly in Deutschland and partly in Holland. Back in medieval times, the Frisians did not have a large cavalry, so they needed to protect their villages with these barriers."

"You are correct, Mr. Bauer. These logs with many long wooden spikes projecting from them will keep the Santee horses from getting too close to the house. The warriors could dismount and possibly climb over them, but it would be slow, and they would be sitting ducks for our bullets and arrows."

"Colonel Sibley has probably sent cavalry troops who will be passing by here on their way to New Ulm. He is following them at a slower pace with infantry and artillery. Both John and I are scouts for the U.S. Army now and will be ordered to surveille the Santee and monitor their progress. But I have a hunch that in the next two days the Santee will be here again with a much larger war party. John and I talked it over, and once he returns, both of us will stay here to help defend you."

"In the meantime, we must be ready to fight off the next attack. It could happen any time now."

"Ja, we will be ready! Karl and Wilhelm, go collect all the arrows and crossbow bolts that are spread about in the yard and bring them back here. We will need every one of these projectiles in the next fight. *Schnell*!"

‚ÄìÔúÅÔúÅÔúÅ‚Äì

CHAPTER FIFTEEN

Chief Little Crow called a meeting of his warriors late at night, the day of Snowy Owl's defeat at the Perrault farm. He stood up in the middle of a circle of two hundred-plus warriors to inspire them for the coming days. "Today we began our war to drive the white settlers out of our ancestral lands. The white man with his farms has scared away the deer and the herds of buffalo that we hunt and eat. And now we find ourselves hunting rabbits and squirrels, and you know how many rabbits and squirrels it takes to feed a hungry family! The white man has pushed us into reservations with the promise of payments to buy food from them at the agencies. But this year they have not delivered the payments and have turned us away from their stores of food, telling us to eat grass! Our children are in danger of starving because of what the white man has done!"

"Your raids into the white man's farmland were mostly successful and have brought us much-needed meat and other food. And you have killed many white men and brought back their wives and daughters as captives. We will hold these creatures as hostages, and the white man must pay for their return. So don't impregnate them or disfigure them or the white man will not want them back!"

"Tomorrow we must attack the white man's village, New Ulm, where many of the white people have fled for safety. We will show them that there is no place where they might be safe!

These particular white men are weak and believe in a god who could not even defend himself from being killed. We will defeat them easily. Kill the men and boys. Remember, don't kill the women and girls. Kill the men first and then if a woman or girl looks good to you, you may bring her back as a concubine."

"I will personally lead you into battle tomorrow morning. We will strike them at dawn while many of them are still sleeping. Every warrior will be needed -- there will not be time for raids against individual farms. We must destroy New Ulm before the horse soldiers arrive."

Of course, both Roaring Cloud and Snowy Owl had different ideas than Little Crow. Roaring Cloud wanted revenge against both John Other Day and Robert, and Snowy Owl wanted to kill Robert and take Little Fox for his own. Glancing at each other as the warriors disbanded from the meeting, they understood each other's intentions; then they decided to set aside their differences to form a raiding party at the tail end of Little Crow's column of warriors. Between them, they were able to enlist the aid of thirty young warriors, all eager to collect scalps.

The next morning at first light, the warriors gathered their weapons and mounted their horses. Snowy Owl and Roaring Cloud and their band of warriors brought up the rear of the column riding to New Ulm. As the column of warriors, now about three-hundred strong, passed the Perrault farm, Snowy Owl motioned to his breakaway band to slow down and stop once the farmhouse was no longer in sight. Then after a time calculated to make the defenders think they would not be attacked, Snowy Owl planned to lead the warriors back to attack the Perrault farm, but this time without the usual war whoops. The element of surprise could work well to their advantage.

When Henri and Blue Feather noticed the column of three hundred warriors approaching the Perrault farm on the way to

New Ulm, they felt a moment of terror, because there was no way the farm could be defended against a force that large. Henri snapped out of his reverie and rang the bell alerting everyone to stand ready with their weapons. Mr. Bauer took his position at the repeating crossbow, next to Henri with his air rifle, and next to him Makawee took up her bow. At ground level were Robert with his Colt six-gun, Silver Wolf with his bow and rifle, Blue Feather with his bow and rifle, and Yung Wing with his bow and sword. But then the column of warriors galloped past them in the direction of New Ulm.

"It looks like it was not our turn today," Henri called down to Blue Feather. But Blue Feather urged caution, "Let's not let down our guard -- stay alert everyone!"

Then they waited until the point where they felt foolish for waiting, and they began to set down their weapons. And that's when Snowy Owl's thirty-one warriors came galloping back to launch their attack.

Once again, the gate to the farm homestead was locked; in fact, it was locked in six places! Jumping over the fence was not an option because it was too high for the horses. Two Santee warriors dismounted to try to hack off the locks with their tomahawks, leaving themselves plain targets for the long-range bullets of Henri, and the arrows of Makawee, Blue Feather, and Silver Wolf. The mounted warriors tried to answer arrows with their arrows, but because their horses were jittery and moving, their aim tended to be off target.

After losing four warriors to the long-range weapons, the Santee war party finally broke through and attempted a full-frontal assault, shooting madly at the defenders at the farmhouse. But they found that they had to pull up short when they saw the Frisian horses. However, one rider didn't stop and tried to urge his horse to jump over the barricade. Unfortunately, the horse was smarter than the rider in this instance, and the horse came to a sudden stop. The surprised rider flew over the horse's head and impaled himself on the pointed sticks. He was grunting in pain, clearly mortally wounded. Yung Wing ran up to him and ended his suffering with his sword.

The Santee liked to fight man-to-man because they wanted to count coup which brought them honor. It involved striking the enemy by hand or with a weapon or simply with a coup stick. One warrior made a daring attempt to climb over the barricade but was shot dead by Karl Bauer who stood at the open farmhouse door. Robert looked back at him and called out,

"Great shot, Karl! But don't stand there in the wide open! Duck back behind the wall after you shoot!"

But just after he said this, an arrow came flying in and pierced Karl's side, or so it appeared. Frau Bauer screamed as she saw Karl stagger away from the door, with an arrow sticking through his side. *"Oh mein Gott! Lieber Gott im Himmel, bitte lass meinen Jungen nicht sterben!"* (Oh my god! Dear God in heaven, please don't let my boy die!)

Little Fox ran up with a kitchen chair, "Karl, sit down here!" Mrs. Bauer gingerly removed Karl's shirt as Little Fox ran to the kitchen to get a bowl of water from the pitcher poured earlier in the day, and a bottle of whiskey.

"Mrs. Bauer, I have dealt with arrow wounds in my Indian village many times. Let me take a look at Karl's wound," said Little Fox as she knelt beside Karl. "Fortunately, the arrow did not hit an artery or pierce any organs. It simply dug a groove in your flesh."

Then Roseanne hurried into the room, "May I have a look? Oh, yes! You are fortunate, young man. But take a drink of this to ease the pain," she said holding out a mug with whiskey.

"The next thing we must do is remove the arrow. You are very fortunate that the arrowhead did not embed itself in your body. I can just ease out the arrow very gently like this." Karl gritted his teeth and resisted the urge to cry out. Nonetheless, tears welled up in his eyes.

"Now we must clean the wound and apply pressure to stop the bleeding," said Roseanne.

Meanwhile, the ground-level defenders mowed down several more as the Santee had to stop short at the barricade. Robert fired his six-gun until he had to reload, killing one warrior and wounding a second. Blue Feather shot arrow after arrow, striking down two warriors, and Yung Wing did the same.

Even after killing or wounding eleven warriors, there were still twenty left, and they didn't look like they were going to retreat. Henri was beginning to lose heart when he heard the cavalry bugle!

A company of mounted infantry (dragoons) led by John Other Day stormed down the same road taken by Little Crow's warriors an hour before. Immediately upon arrival at the Perrault farm, they dismounted and began firing at will. Eight more Santee braves were killed or wounded seriously, and the twelve warriors remaining, which included Snowy Eagle and Roaring Cloud, retreated with haste, galloping off in the direction of New Ulm. The company of dragoons gave chase.

Roaring Cloud rode with the warriors until he could no longer see the Perrault farm. Then he let the warriors ride on as he steered his horse into the woods that stretched for a couple of miles parallel to the frontage of the Perrault farm. Finding a thick tree to hide behind, he dismounted and tethered his horse to a branch, to spy on the Perrault farm using field glasses he stole from a farmer on a previous raid. He planned to wait until John Other Day dared to appear outside alone, preferably by the entrance to the farm. Roaring Cloud was resolved to kill the man who humiliated him some weeks in the past.

Roaring Cloud waited for hours for John Other Day to appear alone. He counted eleven people staying at the farm with most of the men moving and piling up the fallen Santee warriors. Two boys were collecting arrows and bolts from the dead. The women seemed busy inside the home, probably cooking for the men. And then everyone seemed to be taking turns using the outhouse. Roaring Cloud was getting increasingly impatient as sunset would not be more than an hour away.

At that point, Roaring Cloud had an odd feeling that someone was standing behind him. He turned and there stood John Other Day and Blue Feather!

"What? How did you sneak up on me?!

"Roaring Cloud, I already had been a warrior for twenty-five years before you were even born," said John.

And Blue Feather added, "This isn't my first rodeo, either. We noticed you observing the farmhouse and decided to enter these woods on opposite sides and flank you."

"It should be obvious, but we are here to arrest you, and tomorrow morning we'll take you to Fort Ridgely where you will stand trial," said John Other Day.

"Now, throw down your knife."

"A Santee warrior does not answer to white man's laws!" said Roaring Cloud as he rapidly drew his blade and lunged at John Other Day. But John was anticipating trouble and he was able to sidestep Roaring Cloud's knife and drew his weapon, a Bowie knife with a foot-long blade.

"Are you sure you want to fight me?"

"I will fight you and kill you!" said Roaring Cloud as he began to move in a circle around his opponent.

Suddenly he lunged at John's midsection; but again, John dodged his knife. But this time he sliced downward to cut Roaring Cloud's hand. Roaring Cloud screamed and dropped his knife, then ran to where his war club was resting. He ran at John swinging his club wildly. John kept moving backward until he was nearly against a large tree. Roaring Cloud swung again only to strike the tree, jarring the war club from his hands. John then punched his attacker hard on the chin and he fell backward onto the ground, apparently knocked unconscious.

Blue Feather and John looked at each other with some confusion, because he wasn't hit that hard. Blue Feather stooped to turn over Roaring Cloud and that is when they noticed he had opened his skull by falling on a heavy stone with a pointed ridge on top. Roaring Cloud was dead.

"Oh my God! I didn't mean to kill him!"

"I know, John, I know. But remember, he was trying to kill you. You could have killed him earlier if you had wanted."

"We should bury him here, but first I must get a shovel. I'll go get one and I'll bury him tonight."

"I'll go with you and carry a lantern back with us, so we can see what we are doing."

When they returned, they buried Roaring Cloud using the stone that killed him as a headstone. Somehow that seemed an appropriate ending to this episode.

Sighing, Blue Feather turned to John Other Day and said, "John, I suppose now I must return to Colonel Sibley and report for duty. How about you?"

John did not immediately reply, being lost in his thoughts. After a few seconds he said, "I deeply regret killing this young man. He was not a good man, but could have been, had he only opened his heart to Jesus. But it makes no sense to dwell on this. As it so happens, I also must return to Colonel Sibley and report for duty. So, after we say our goodbyes at the farm, let's ride to New Ulm and see if we find Colonel Sibley still there."

⊙⊙⊙

CHAPTER SIXTEEN

The Santee uprising continued with four hundred Santee warriors led by Little Crow attacking Fort Ridgely. The defenders, consisting of U.S. soldiers and armed civilians, were able to repulse the Santee.

Next, the Santees attacked the town of New Ulm. The town's population had swollen to two thousand from the original nine hundred. Although only about three hundred civilians were armed, the Santees were forced to retreat. The Santee forces returned to Fort Ridgely and again were unsuccessful. They returned to New Ulm with more than six hundred Santee warriors led by Chiefs Waŋbdiṭanka, Wabaśa, and Mankato. But once more the Santee failed.

After the second unsuccessful attack, Charles Flandreau, elected as the military commander, oversaw the evacuation of the two thousand residents of New Ulm and outlying areas, leading them to Mankato, St. Peter, and St. Paul. A column of refugees stretched over four miles with people carrying what they could of their possessions on their backs.

Overnight the towns of Mankato and St. Peter turned into refugee camps, with people jamming into hastily assembled shelters. With crowding and poor sanitation, diseases quickly passed from person to person. As weakened adults and children succumbed to the diseases, more lives were lost.

ᏽᏽᏽᏽ

As the Santee began to concentrate their attacks on New Ulm and Fort Ridgely, and other towns, Henri felt that the risk to the Perrault farm was diminishing somewhat and persons on that farm began to return to their normal daily activities. John Other Day was still serving as a scout for Colonel Sibley. This left five men protecting the Perrault farm: Henri, Yung Wing, Mr. Bauer, Robert, and Silver Wolf. But Robert and Silver Wolf were feeling restless and perhaps even embarrassed that they were not doing more to put down the Santee rebellion. Robert thought he should talk to his family about joining Colonel Sibley's forces. He especially felt the need to do something with the news that a band of Santee warriors had attacked a supply wagon carrying new weapons to Fort Ridgely. The threat to the white settlers in the Minnesota River valley substantially increased with more warriors armed with rifles. It might even tip the balance in favor of the Santee.

At Fort Ridgely after the retreat of the Santee warriors, John Other Day was granted a couple of days of leave from his duties as a scout for Colonel Sibley, and he used it to visit his family. He rode through the night and arrived at the Perrault farm around sunrise. Everyone was already up and having their breakfast provided by the ladies. When John rode up on his black stallion, Roseanne jumped up to hug and greet him followed by Makawee and Linda Marie (Little Fox had reverted to the name her parents had given her at birth to honor their memory). After all the hugs and kisses, Roseanne had her husband sit down and she served him breakfast, which he enthusiastically consumed.

"Oh, this is so much better than camp food! I can't tell you how much I missed your cooking, Roseanne!"

The men took their conversation outdoors so that they could discuss the war. They walked the perimeter of the homestead.

"Is there any sign of this war ending soon, John?" asked Henri. John looked away for a second and then said, "Well, I was thinking that the fighting would be ending soon, but yesterday, we found out that a supply wagon carrying new rifles for our troops was attacked by a band of Santee warriors. The wagon was guarded by Captain Marsh himself and six mounted infantrymen. They were ambushed and killed -- every one of them. There were thirty rifles and ammunition on that wagon. Most were Enfields but two of the rifles were Whitworths."

"Whitworths! Oh my gosh -- that is a long-distance sniper weapon capable of hitting targets at eight hundred to one thousand yards! Will the Santee have any warrior who can effectively use this weapon?"

"Henri, there are warriors who are skilled marksmen with less refined rifles. So, I don't think it will be long before they catch on that this weapon is useful for sniping. The only thing that might diminish their enthusiasm is their concept of counting coup."

"Oh right, that is their way of keeping score and of showing mastery over their enemies. And then the scalp is the trophy they carry home with them."

"Yes, you have that right."

၅၅၅၅

At this point, Robert and his friend Silver Wolf walked up to Henri and John hoping to get their approval to join the militia to fight the rebelling Santee.

"Pa, we want to talk to you about joining the militia. Grandfather, we also request your wisdom."

Henri and John looked at each other. John could see the concerned look on Henri's face.

"So, you want to join the militia and fight under Colonel Sibley? Is that what you are telling me? You both understand that this is a dangerous thing to do?"

"Yes, Pa. But we figure it's far more dangerous for those people who aren't prepared to fight and defend themselves. The sooner this war ends, the better."

"And Silver Wolf, you would not regret fighting against Santee warriors, your tribesmen, including some young men you grew up with?" asked John.

"My allegiance is first to Jesus Christ, not the Santee nation. I love my people but hate the violence and cruelty some of them are inflicting on my new brothers and sisters. I must try to put an end to this."

"You fellows know that two more soldiers won't make all that much difference in this war, but the two of you make a huge difference to your families. If you lose your lives, think of all the grief your families will suffer," said John.

"I think I speak for both Silver Wolf and myself when I say that we don't want to cause our loved ones any grief, but we can't sit by idly while other families are losing their fathers and sons, and their mothers and daughters are being dragged into captivity."

"What Robert says is true. And it seems to me that the Santee tribe has been especially cruel in this war, killing children and even babies. We must end this war now."

Henri sighed, resigning himself to the decision the young men were making. "Well, I guess there is no point in resisting this -- you are adults now and your minds are made up. Robert, you need to break this news to the others in the family now, and I would start with Linda Marie."

John agreed, "I think your father is right. And when I return to the U.S. Army, the two of you should come with me and be mustered into the service."

☙☙☙

The young men walked back to the farmhouse and had their own conversation.

"Robert, I don't envy you having to tell Little Fox, I mean Linda Marie, of your decision," said Silver Wolf.

"I know what you mean. It will be hard for her to accept, but I believe we are doing the right thing."

Robert and Silver Wolf didn't notice Linda Marie walking up to them until she asked, "What will be hard for me to accept? What are you boys talking about?"

Robert blushed and stammered a bit and before he could say anything, Silver Wolf said, "The two of you need some privacy so I'll go back to my chores," and walked away.

"Now, Robert, out with it! What will be hard for me to accept?" Robert took Linda Marie into his arms and held her for a few seconds taking in her scent and kissing her cheeks and neck.

"Silver Wolf and I are joining the militia to help end this war. We'll leave with Grandfather when he returns to the Army and be mustered into the service."

"No, Robert, no! You could be killed! I love you and I can't lose you! No, no, no!"

"Oh, sweet Linda Marie -- you know how much I love you! But I feel compelled to help end this terrible war. Yes, I might be killed. But think of all the families who have lost their fathers and sons, or their mothers and daughters who have been taken as captives. And think of all the babies that the Santee warriors have killed. I cannot remain here and let these horrible things happen! I don't think any Christian man who can fight should stay out of this war."

Robert looked at Linda Marie barely able to swallow because of a huge lump in his throat. Tears were streaming from her eyes, and at first, she pushed away from his embrace, angry with him. But then she saw his eyes welling up and she threw herself into his arms and the two of them embraced for several seconds. She took her head from his shoulder and looked up at him, "You are a good and noble Christian man, Robert. I won't stand in your way when you want to do God's will!" With that, she left his embrace and ran to Roseanne. Roseanne asked, "Whatever is wrong, Linda Marie?" Linda Marie sobbed and said quietly, "Robert is going to join the Army and go to war!" Just then, Makawee joined them, dismayed when she heard the news. Soon the three women were hugging in a circle. Mrs. Bauer, hearing the commotion, walked up and asked,

"Dear sisters, what has happened?" When they told her the news, she said, "Let us stop crying *und geben wir Robert in die Hände Gottes. Ach!* I mean to say, put Robert into the hands of God." And then she offered up a prayer, to which all said amen.

Later in the day, Henri called Robert into his workshop. John, Mr. Bauer, and Jung Wing were there also. "Robert, if you are mature enough to go to war, you are mature enough to get married!"

Robert's eyes widened and he nearly collapsed in shock. The men chuckled at his reaction.

"But I don't have a ring to give her!"

Henri held up a simple gold wedding ring, "This belonged to my mother. You can make it Linda Marie's!"

"But there isn't a minister nearby who can perform the ceremony."

"Not true, Herr Robert! I am authorized to preside over weddings by the German Brethren Church," said a smiling Mr. Bauer.

"But we don't have a home of our own."

"Robert, I am moving on after this war is over. You can have my room in this workshop," said Jung Wing.

"And later this fall, assuming the war is over, you can help me build a house that is attached to the workshop," said Henri.

"But I don't have a job! How would I support her?"

"Robert, you have been my apprentice for more than a year as both a gunsmith and a locksmith; plus, you can have a share of the farm! Son, the most important questions are these: do you love her, and do you feel like you could find someone better?"

"I love her with all my heart and there could not be anyone better for me!"

"Then, son, I suggest that you propose marriage to Linda Marie as soon as possible," said Henri.

"And I urge you to have the wedding tomorrow because in two days we must report back at Fort Ridgely," said Robert's grandfather, John.

"Oh boy, I'm getting dizzzzzy..." said Robert who started to collapse. But Henri caught him, and Jung Wing ran over with a chair. "I think he needs a good strong drink," said John, who poured some whiskey into a mug. Robert drank some and shook his head, "What is this stuff?"

Henri said, "Some call it liquid courage. Now, go find Linda Marie and propose to her."

Robert took the ring and put it into his shirt pocket then he walked to the farmhouse where he heard the women talking and in the kitchen. He mustered his courage, and walked in and said, "Linda Marie, would you walk with me? Without saying a word, Linda Marie took Robert's hand and left the other women, but looked back at them briefly and saw that they were all smiling. Their reaction was a little puzzling to her, but she shook it off.

They walked to the big shade tree where Henri had built a park bench. Robert said, "Please sit down here." And as she sat down, Robert took a deep breath and knelt on one knee and took her hand. "Linda Marie, I love you, you are precious to me, and I can't imagine life without you! Will you marry me?" And reaching into his shirt pocket he held out his father's mother's ring.

For a fraction of a second Linda Marie was speechless, but then she stood up pulling Robert up with her. Jumping into his arms she said, "Yes, of course, I'll marry you!" Then the two lovers kissed passionately.

The wedding took place the next day with Mr. Bauer performing the simple ceremony that the German Brethren Church prescribed. He faltered at points as he translated the words from his prayer book into English from High German, but that didn't matter to anyone, because all eyes were on the handsome young couple. Robert wore a black suit with a tie for the first time, and Linda Marie wore a white bridal gown that had belonged to Makawee.

They spent their wedding night in a teepee John Other Day and Silver Wolf had erected in the farmyard. The teepee provided some privacy, but the irony of the situation was not lost on them. And after getting over their shyness, Robert and Linda Marie made passionate love.

ᏬᏬᏬ

CHAPTER SEVENTEEN

The second day after the wedding there were tearful good-byes as John, his grandson Robert, and Robert's friend Silver Wolf prepared to saddle their stallions and ride off to report at Fort Ridgely.

"I promise you, Linda Marie, that this will all work out for good. Remember what the angel told me, 'God has heard your prayers and has sent me to tell you that he has plans for you, plans to prosper you and not to harm you, plans to give you hope and a future. But soon you will experience a period of tumult, war, and suffering. But you and your family will be protected and come through this trial unscathed.' We must have faith!"

"I don't think my faith is as strong as yours is, Robert! Oh Lord, help my unbelief!"

After a long kiss, Robert swung upon his paint, nodded to his grandfather, and the three of them, John, Robert, and Silver Wolf, trotted off in the direction of Fort Ridgely.

Colonel Sibley watched John Other Day return through the gates of the fort. Interestingly, he had two young men with him.

"John Other Day, who are these young men? Have you brought new scouts for enlistment?" said Colonel Sibley.

"Not exactly sir. Allow me to introduce Robert Perrault, my grandson, and his friend, Silver Wolf. Both men are interested in serving as soldiers in the battle against the Santee."

"Is that so? Well, we can always use men who are experienced fighters. Robert, I have heard how your family and friends repulsed an attack by a war party of fifteen braves. I see that you have a Colt 51 revolving pistol and a wood stock that attaches. Are you also handy with a rifle such as an Enfield?"

"Colonel, my father is a gunsmith among other things, and I am his apprentice. We have fixed Enfield rifles among many others, and I have a lot of practice shooting them."

"Excellent! And you, young man, Silver Wolf, is it? You will have no compunctions about fighting men of your tribe?"

Silver Wolf appeared confused, "Compunctions?"

Robert said, "He means you won't feel guilty or ashamed about fighting another Santee?"

"Oh! Colonel, if someone is trying to kill me or my fellow soldiers, I will not hesitate to fight back."

"Well, young men. Come with me to Sergeant McNulty, our quartermaster. He will swear you in and issue you your uniforms. No, on second thought, I think Robert, we will issue you a uniform; but Silver Wolf, we will make you a scout. And it would be better for you to be dressed as a Sioux."

Moments later Sergeant McNulty took one look at Robert and said, "What are you doing out of uniform, Private McMahon? Did something happen to your uniform that you are not wearing it?"

"Sergeant, I'm Robert Perrault, a new recruit to the Army. Today is my first day here!"

Other soldiers collected around Robert and the sergeant and looked on in confusion.

"That's not McMahon. He's working in the stables. I'll go get him," offered one soldier.

"Maybe you are McMahon's twin brother, right?" asked another soldier.

"No, I haven't even met McMahon yet."

A minute later, the soldier returned with Private Patrick McMahon, and the circle of soldiers around them grew tighter, and they shared their observations.

"The new recruit is about a half-inch taller."

"They look like they're about the same weight."

"Their hair is about the same! And both have blue eyes. Are you sure you're not related?"

Robert said to Patrick, "I can see why these guys would think we're related, but we're not even close to being twins!"

"Well, all I know is that if I'm caught doing something I should not be doing, I'm going to say that I am you, from now on!" said Patrick with a playful smile.

"Well, then -- I'll do the same!

Patrick offered his hand, "I'm Patrick McMahon. My father is Irish, and my mother is half Sauk Indian and half French."

"And I'm Robert Perrault. My father is French, and my mother is three-quarters Sioux and Ojibwa and one-quarter English."

"So, we're both mixed-bloods!" they said in unison.

In the next few days, Silver Wolf was sent out with John Other Day on a scouting mission, and they did not return until late the next day. In the meantime, Patrick was selected to go with a twelve-man squad of soldiers to Fort Snelling to pick up ammunition and transfer it to Fort Ridgely. Impressed with his skills, Colonel Sibley kept Robert at the Fort to train the still green soldiers on marksmanship and man-to-man combat.

Little Crow had ordered Snowy Owl to surveil the fort from the cover of trees some two hundred yards away. When a large empty wagon left the fort with twelve mounted soldiers, Snowy Owl watched with great interest, taking note of their direction away from the fort. Once he had confirmed in his mind which direction they were headed, and they had ridden out of sight, Snowy Owl galloped back to Little Crow with his report.

"Father, the soldiers have sent an empty wagon from Fort Ridgely in the direction of Fort Snelling. I figure they are going to Fort Snelling to pick up ammunition. If we can stop them on their return trip, we can claim the ammunition for ourselves."

Little Crow nodded, "Then take twenty or so warriors with you and set up an ambush. Take one of those Whitworth rifles and cut down a few soldiers while they are still distant. Then swoop in with your war party and kill them, all of them!"

When the time came for the ambush, Snowy Owl and his war party were ready and waiting. Snowy Owl had claimed the privilege of firing the Whitworth rifle. Using the field glasses he had stolen from some white farmer, Snowy Owl scanned the faces of the soldiers as they approached the ambush site. His heart skipped a beat when he spotted Robert riding alongside the wagon. He knew then which soldier would be his first target!

Snowy Owl lined up his target in his sights, held his breath, and then squeezed the trigger. A second later, he observed Robert falling off his horse, apparently dead. The shot from the Whitworth was the signal for the twenty Santee braves to swoop down on the soldiers. The battle did not last long with the eleven soldiers facing the twenty-one Santee braves. Every soldier was killed and then scalped. Snowy Owl made sure that he scalped Robert. He would need the distinctive scalp to convince Little Fox that her half-breed lover was dead. His possession of the scalp would prove that he, Snowy Owl, was the superior warrior. As Snowy Owl bent over Robert to begin the grisly business of scalping him, he hesitated a moment but then remembered that Robert was the man who had alienated Little

Fox from him. He spat out, "You should have stayed away from her!" and then he scalped his victim.

Two riderless horses ran back to the safety of Fort Ridgely. There was no doubt in Colonel Sibley's mind what this meant. Shortly afterward, John Other Day and Silver Wolf returned from their reconnaissance mission. They reported that a large number of Santee were moving in a northwesterly direction up the Minnesota River valley toward Lone Tree or Battle Lake. Colonel Sibley said in response, "I guess that is where we will find our ammunition wagon. I am going to telegraph the acting commander at Ft. Snelling and request that we combine forces and meet the enemy with overwhelming numbers to eliminate these troublemakers once and for all!"

By early September, the tide of the war had turned to the advantage of the U.S. Army. Colonel Sibley (soon to be Brigadier General), after the battle of Birch Coulee, believed that the Santee had grown weary of the war, and he began to communicate with Chief Little Crow. Chief Little Crow wrote to the general:

"For what reason we have commenced this war, I will tell you. We made a treaty with the government, and beg for what we do get, and can't get that till our children are dying from hunger. It is the traders who commenced it. Mr. A.J. Myrick told the Indians that they would eat grass or dirt. Then Mr. Forbes told the Lower Sioux that they were not men. Then Forbes was working with his friends to defraud us out of our money..."

Little Crow indicated that he would negotiate with Col. Sibley for the release of several hundred white hostages, but Col. Sibley would not negotiate, and instead demanded that the Sioux surrender. Little Crow would not surrender, and so the stage was set for another battle.

The death toll caused the war-weary chiefs to give up their white hostages at what became known as Camp Release. Many Santee warriors surrendered, but enough remained to wage one more battle.

ᎣᎣᎣ

CHAPTER EIGHTEEN

The Abduction

One morning after breakfast, on the porch of the Perrault home, Elfriede Bauer gazed longingly in the direction of her home, the next farm to the north. Linda Marie observed her for a moment and decided to ask her what she was thinking about. "Mrs. Bauer, is everything all right with you? What are you thinking about?"

"I am thinking about mein haus, wondering if anything is salvageable there, like mein china, silverware, cooking pots und pans. Die Indianer destroyed most everything, I suppose, when they burned down das haus, but I am curious."

"Well, things are peaceful now; why don't we hitch up your buckboard and go find out?"

"*Die Männer sind alle in der Werkstatt und es wird Stunden dauern, bis wir anfangen müssen, das Abendessen zu kochen.* Ach, let me say that in English. The menfolk are all in the workshop and it will be hours before we need to begin *kochen* the evening meal."

"So, let's go!" said Linda Marie with a smile.

The two women hitched the Bauer's farm horse, Brunhilde, to the buckboard wagon and trotted over to the Bauer farm, about nine-tenths of a mile away. Once there, they began picking through the ruins of the Bauers' home. It did not look like there would be much to salvage, and tears welled up in Elfriede's eyes. Linda Marie turned to hug and comfort her. As the two

127

women embraced, four Santee warriors silently stepped into the ruins coming from the other side of the tall fireplace/chimney, the only part of the farmhouse that remained standing. They quickly sprang on the women, pushing them to the floor, laying astride them, and putting a dirty hand over their mouths. Strong Bear was on top of Elfriede who was desperately fighting to get free, but Strong Bear was quite heavy and lived up to his name.

White Eagle stepped over to hold down her arms, and Strong Bear just laughed at her efforts to free herself, "Ah, this one is strong and pretty, and has a lot of fire in her; and just look at these hips!" and he ran his hands appraisingly over her body. "She would give her man strong sons." Elfriede screamed silently at his touch.

Meanwhile, Snowy Owl put his full weight on Linda Marie while Red Cloud held down her arms. Linda Marie's eyes showed her indignation, but then something on Snowy Owl's belt caught her attention, and now her eyes showed terror. "Oh, you see this scalp? Yes, it belongs to that half-breed lover of yours! I defeated him easily in battle, which only proves what I have been saying -- that I am the superior warrior. Well, now you belong to me, and I will take you to my teepee."

Linda Marie went limp with grief and Snowy Owl and Red Cloud wasted no time in gagging her and tying her hands and ankles.

Snowy Owl glanced over at Elfriede. "Strong Bear, are you going to take that blondie with you, or have her here? You don't need her; you have both a squaw and a white concubine already."

Strong Bear let down his guard for a moment and knelt on one knee, looking at Snowy Owl. Elfriede saw an opportunity to deliver a hard kick to Strong Bear's groin and he fell over grunting in pain. The other warriors just laughed at him, and Snowy Owl said, "Well, I guess you're not going to have her here!"

Strong Bear recovered somewhat and hit Elfriede hard on the face, stunning her. "No, she is not worth the effort. There's too much fight in this one! Let's tie her up and just leave her here."

The warriors unhitched Brunhilde from the buckboard wagon and tied Linda Marie to her, draping her face down over the beast like a horse blanket and connecting her wrists to her ankles by means of a rope running under the horse.

"Sorry Little Fox, the buckboard might have been more comfortable, but we must return quickly to our camp and avoid the horse soldiers," said Snowy Owl in a mocking tone.

Thinking that she was unconscious, the warriors left Elfriede lying in a heap on the floor of her ruined home. She watched which direction the raiding party was taking. It was a north-westerly direction, she was sure of that. When they were out of sight, she scooted to the fireplace to rub the rope binding her hands against the corner of the fireplace. It was a slow process, but she eventually freed herself. She ungagged herself and found a stone to rub against the rope binding her ankles -- it had been tied too tightly for her to untie. Once free, she stood up unsteadily. Her face still smarted where she had been struck, and her ribs felt like they had been bruised. But she was resolved to return to the Perrault farm as soon as possible. She started to walk, first quite painfully. Then after praying for strength, she built up speed.

Mr. Bauer was just stepping outside when Elfriede staggered up to the gate of the Perrault farm. He was shocked to see her in this condition and ran to her.

"Oh du meine Güte, was ist mit dir passiert? Bist du ernsthaft verletzt, und war Linda Marie bei dir?" [Oh, my goodness, what has happened to you? Are you seriously hurt? And was Linda Marie with you?"]

"It was terrible! Linda Marie and I were at our old farmhouse looking for anything salvageable when four Indian warriors tackled us and lay upon us. They tied our ankles and hands together and gagged us. They decided they didn't want me and so I was left there. But Linda Marie knew one of them and it seemed that he had come specifically for her. The Indian she knew showed her a scalp hanging from his belt, and he must have said it was Robert's. I don't know for certain what they were saying because they were speaking in their Sioux language. Oh, but it did look like Robert's! And she cried, Ach, did she ever cry!"

"Did you see which direction they took?"

"Yes, they rode in a northwesterly direction."

Mr. Bauer picked up his wife and carried her into the house as she wept. Makawee and Roseanne walked quickly into the room, as Mr. Bauer set his wife down in a chair.

"What has happened? Where is Linda Marie?" asked Roseanne.

Mr. Bauer held up his hand, "Please, Elfriede cannot speak right now. I will tell you what has happened but first let's get everyone together. Karl, please go get Henri and Yung Wing. Tell them it is an emergency."

Once everyone was assembled, Mr. Bauer told them what Elfriede had told him.

"The Indian she knew must have been Snowy Owl! And the scalp he had attached to his belt could have been Robert's!" said Makawee, who then broke into a sob.

Henri embraced his wife and said, "Makawee, we must not give up hope! Remember what the angel told Robert in his vision quest -- that there would be tumult and war, but that our family would emerge from it unharmed. I must go after these abductors and rescue Linda Marie and find out the truth about Robert. Yung Wing, will you come with me?"

"Henri, there is no way you could keep me from helping you."

"Mr. Bauer, the women need a man to stay here and protect them. Otherwise, I'd ask you to come as well."

"I understand! I will stay here and defend this household."

"There will be two men here to defend this household, my father and me," said Karl.

Henri smiled and said, "Thank you, Karl. You are indeed a brave and capable young man."

"Yung Wing, let's collect our weapons, throw together some provisions, saddle up and go!"

Flora Belle and Nancy were hardly warhorses, but they were the only steeds to choose from. Claude and Samson were mules and had never been ridden. Flora Belle had been ridden more than Nancy, so Henri chose her. Yung Wing still had his gelding, Free Spirit, which he had ridden from California to Minnesota.

"Fortunate for us, it rained last night, and the ground was still soft. The unshod horses ridden by the four Santee should be easy enough to find and track," said Henri.

"Yes, and perhaps by the spacing of the hoofprints we can tell what speed they were going."

"It appears that this party of four was heading toward the lakes, maybe Wood Lake or Lone Tree Lake."

"Perhaps this is the new collection point for the Santee. They have abandoned their original village."

"And perhaps this is the new staging area for launching their next series of attacks."

"I'll bet that John has already figured this out as a scout for Colonel Sibley; but if our trail takes us anywhere near Fort Ridgely, we should stop there to share our discovery and see if the Colonel will reinforce us with some mounted troops in our recovery of Linda Marie."

After the families gathered for prayer, Henri and Yung Wing galloped off and headed toward the Bauer farm to pick up the trail. As Henri looked back, he could see Roseanne and Makawee embracing each other and kneeling in prayer.

∽∽∽∽

Snowy Owl and his three accomplices arrived at the new camp. The four of them carried Linda Marie to Snowy Owl's teepee and set her down. Her hands and ankles were still tied.

"Enjoy yourself with your new squaw, Snowy Owl," said Strong Bear with a leer. Red Cloud and White Eagle just snickered as they crept out of the teepee.

Snowy Owl figured he should get right down to business, so he took off his shirt. Linda Marie started to sob and plead with him not to violate her. She tried to crawl away from him, but he sat astride her and ran his hands over her body. Just at that moment, two women hurried into the tent and began to strike Snowy Owl on the back with switches. One was his mother, and the other was the former mistress of Little Fox.

"Is this the way you behave with a bride? She does not want you if you must force yourself on her."

"Did you capture her on a raid? This is Little Fox who was my daughter and servant for most of her life. If she had wanted to be your squaw, the two of you would have been married by now."

"Yes, I stole her back from that white man's farm, where the half breed lived. On a separate occasion, I killed her lover, the half-breed. She belongs to me now."

"You killed her husband, that nice boy who used to come to our village? That ring on her finger is the way the whites show that a woman is married."

After he nodded yes, the women began beating him all over again. "You will not sleep with her while she mourns her husband. Now get out of here and do not bother her again."

Stinging from the beating he had just taken, and painfully humiliated by a pair of women, Snowy Owl made his way to his father's teepee and spent the night there.

The next morning Little Crow discussed his plans with Snowy Owl. "Forces are collecting now for what I think will be the final battle between the Santee Sioux and the federal soldiers. We are likely to lose this battle. The federal army will bring cannons along with more soldiers than we have faced before. If we lose, the Santee Sioux will be rounded up and imprisoned. I don't want that for my family. So, we are going to escape before that happens. Have your woman bound and gagged if you must, but we will leave once the battle is engaged. I never wanted this war, and I warned severely against it, so now when the white man seeks his revenge, it is not right for me or my family to be subjected to it."

"But Father, where will we go?"

"We will head north to Canada. The whites in the U.S. will not cross the imaginary line they call the border to pursue us into Canada. There are Sioux villages in Canada where we can live."

There had been some frustrating delays in what would become the final battle of the war. It took nine days to march 1,400 troops, many of whom were inexperienced, from Fort Snelling to Fort Ridgely in the Minnesota River valley; and then when these troops arrived, further delays were experienced in obtaining horses, guns, and ammunition. Finally, on September 19 the troops began their movement up the Minnesota River valley to confront the Santee.

The battle of Wood Lake took place east of Lone Tree Lake, a small lake drained by a creek running northeast to the Minnesota River. General Sibley's guide mistakenly thought that the lake was Wood Lake, which is sixty-nine miles to the northwest. Here the soldiers and the Santee warriors met on the battlefield with the U.S. Army, this time armed with several field cannons. The Santee suffered many casualties including Chief Mankato who was killed by a cannonball.

When the battle looked like it was going to be a decisive defeat for the Santee, Little Crow and Snowy Owl quietly left the battlefield and returned to their new camp. There they loaded up their women, including Little Fox, who was already tied up and gagged. She would make the trip to Canada bound to a travois pulled by the stolen Brunhilde. Several hand-picked warriors and their families were also making the journey thinking that they had been secretly selected to serve as envoys to various Canadian bands of Sioux to recruit their warriors to fight in the war in Minnesota. They were unaware that their real purpose was to serve as armed escorts to get Little Crow safely delivered to Manitoba. They left the camp without disturbing their teepees, so it would look like the men were still fighting in the battle.

Their trek north to where related bands of Sioux were residing in Manitoba was about 250 miles or about 12 days. The group's traveling speed was limited by several travois laden with household goods, clothing, and a few small children. Because they would be traversing Ojibwa territory, Chief Little Crow had scouts forging ahead about a quarter mile in front of the group.

Little Crow advised his followers, "The Ojibwa are traditional enemies, and the presence of Santee Sioux will be construed as an intrusion. Be aware of Ojibwa braves as we pass through what they consider to be their hunting grounds. We have only ten warriors and they could have many more. They might think of us as the first of many Santees who are fleeing the U.S. Army in Minnesota and they would kill us all as a warning to any future intruders."

☽☽☽☽

CHAPTER NINETEEN

The Rescue

Henri and Yung Wing picked up the abductors' trail at the Bauer farm and followed it in a northwesterly direction. After a couple of miles, it seemed to Henri that the four Santee raiders had not changed their direction and were riding at a good clip toward the lakes keeping the Minnesota River on their right.

"There are four unshod horses and one heavier shod horse which I'll bet is Mr. Bauer's farm horse, Brunhilde. This mare is old and not very energetic anymore, and that is fortunate because she will set a slower pace."

After about ten miles, Yung Wing said, "Henri, I have noticed the hoof prints are getting closer together. Brunhilde is tiring and slowing down, forcing the Indian ponies to slow down." After about another six miles, Henri and Yung Wing started to pick up smells that suggested a settlement was nearby. They detected the smell of campfires and livestock. As they continued, they could see teepees beyond a copse of pine trees, and they decided to stealthily approach the camp to observe activity in it. They tied their horses to branches of a tree and crept closer to the camp, peering around trees.

Henri whispered to Yung Wing, "I haven't seen any men, just women, and children. I suppose that means the braves are on raids or..." Henri was cut off by the booms of two cannons. Then he continued, "The braves must be engaged in a battle! It sounded like it is a mile or less to the west of here. Let's mount up and get closer." They rode close enough to observe the battle but not enough to be drawn into it. Then they spotted Colonel Sibley at the rear of the soldiers, and they rode an arc around the battlefield to get to him.

"The Colonel will tell us if Robert was killed by the Santee!" We have to check in with him!" And without delay, they rode up to where he was observing the battle. Henri dismounted quickly and ran up to the Colonel. "Colonel Sibley, sir! I am Henri Perrault, Robert's father..."

Colonel Sibley interrupted Henri, "Oh, yes! Robert Perrault is an excellent young man. He is becoming a fine soldier. You raised him well, Mr. Perrault!"

"Then Robert is alive and well? Oh my gosh, that is a great relief! If you have a couple of minutes, I want to tell you why it is important for Robert to join me and Yung Wing, my companion, in a rescue mission. Early this morning, a raiding party of four Santee abducted Linda Marie, also known as Little Fox, and headed in this general direction. Linda Marie is my son's wife. She must be thinking that she is a widow because her abductor, Snowy Owl, had a scalp that could have been Robert's, and he told her he had killed him in battle."

"That scalp belonged to Patrick McMahon, another young private. Patrick and Robert could have been twin brothers, the resemblance was that close! Mr. Perrault, this is highly irregular, but then nothing in an Indian conflict can go strictly by the book. I'll tell you what -- I will assign Robert, his grandfather John Other Day, Robert's friend Silver Wolf, and my chief scout, Blue Feather, to your rescue party. I will have less need of these men shortly because this battle today could be our very last engagement of the war. The Santees are taking a terrible beating. Two of their chiefs have already fallen. That should take some steam out of this war."

Colonel Sibley then turned to his executive officer, "Captain, spread the word through the troops that I want Robert Perrault, Silver Wolf, John Other Day, and Blue Feather to report to me immediately." The captain then rushed to the nearest non-commissioned officers to start spreading the word.

It took thirty minutes or longer to round up the four men. Colonel Sibley immediately told them the reason for their being summoned, "Men, I am authorizing a rescue mission that involves the Perrault family. I will let Henri Perrault explain the situation."

Henri placed his hand on Robert's shoulder, "Robert, Linda Marie has been abducted by Snowy Owl from the Bauer farm. Linda Marie must be thinking that Snowy Owl killed you because he showed her a scalp that could have been yours. The truth is it was the scalp of Patrick McMahon, which the colonel just now told us. All this happened early this morning. Linda Marie and Elfriede were checking to see if there was anything salvageable. Elfriede was not taken but was beaten and tied up. She pretended to be unconscious and observed that the four raiders rode off in a northwesterly direction. We followed their tracks to the Santee camp close by and then discovered this battlefield."

Robert was stunned by the news. It wasn't part of his nature to fly into a rage, but this news started a fire within him. He was breathing hard and blurted out, "So, we must arm ourselves to the hilt and chase down these heathens and recover Linda Marie. And they must pay for their crime!"

"Son, we will find Linda Marie and punish Snowy Owl and his henchmen for this terrible misdeed," said John Other Day.

"Henri, you should be the leader of this mission," said John Other Day."

"OK, but you know that I have only tracked animals, not men."

"In this case, there is not much difference," said Blue Feather. Don't worry, John and I will advise you if we think you need our counsel."

"Well then, let's mount up and ride to the Santee camp. Blue Feather, since you probably won't be recognized by the Santee who remain in the camp, perhaps you should ride in and ask if anyone has seen Snowy Owl recently. You are fluent in the Sioux language, correct?

"They will think he is a Sioux from a different band, and he will not raise any suspicions whatsoever," said John Other Day. "This is an excellent idea."

The men then rode to the Santee camp, with all but Blue Feather hidden in a copse of maple trees. Blue Feather rode slowly into the camp to ask for the whereabouts of Snowy Owl.

No man was in the camp except for an ancient one who appeared to be deaf or senile. All but one woman said that they had not seen him, and she said that she saw Little Crow and his family and eight young braves including Snowy Owl leave with their women earlier in the day. One of the women was a captive tied to a travois. The rumor in the camp was that they were bound for Canada to recruit warriors from the Sioux bands in Manitoba. The woman who spoke to Blue Feather appeared not to believe that explanation for their departure.

Blue Feather calmly thanked the woman and rode back to where the rest of the posse was waiting. "Little Crow, Snowy Owl, and about eight other young braves are headed north into Manitoba. Linda Marie was tied to a travois. They left a couple of hours ago. Let's see if we can catch up with them so we can just keep them in sight," said Blue Feather.

"But we should have more of a plan going into this. We are outnumbered two to one; we can't directly attack them, so what can we do?" asked Robert.

"I might have a plan, but I want to talk it through with John and Blue Feather. Let's get back on their trail now, and we can talk on the way," said Henri.

The men continued their trek north with Blue Feather and John expertly following the trail of the escaping Santee. It was still warm for late September and the horses needed water and a brief rest, so they stopped at a stream. This allowed Henri to explain his plan.

"You all know the saying 'the enemy of my enemy is my friend.' I don't think it would be wise to assume that this is always true, but in this case, I think we will find allies among the Ojibwa, who are traditional enemies of the Santee Sioux. We need to locate an Ojibwa village and inform them that a Santee Sioux group is violating Ojibwa hunting grounds. Plus, this group of Santee Sioux has taken an Ojibwa girl captive. We might also mention that she is married to a young man who has Ojibwa blood. The goal is to gain their assistance in freeing a young Ojibwa woman from their enemies."

"Will they care about Linda Marie being a captive?" asked Robert.

"They might care if she is related to someone in their clan," suggested John. "Besides, I think I recall what Linda Marie said about her mother's clan. Her mother's clan fished and farmed along the banks of the Mississippi River north of St. Cloud. Their clan's name was the Fish, who were the intellectuals and mediators of the tribe. Hopefully, that means we can reason with them to help us negotiate Linda Marie's release."

"And my mother's Ojibwa clan was the Martens, the warrior clan. They might be especially concerned about a Santee incursion into their territory, and be eager to turn them back," said Robert.

"John and Blue Feather, what do you think of going northeasterly toward the Mississippi River with the hopes of finding an Ojibwa village?

"That is a good idea, Henri," said John.

"Yes, let's get going," said Blue Feather. "And when we approach the Ojibwa village, let me do the talking because I speak their language."

As it turned out, Henri and his posse did not have to look for an Ojibwa village because within a couple of hours a party of twenty-odd Ojibwa warriors crossed their path. As soon as the Ojibwa warriors spotted the posse, they quickly galloped up to them and surrounded them. Their leader spoke for them in French, "This is Ojibwa hunting ground. What are your intentions? If you are not here for trade, you should turn around and return to the south!"

Henri responded in French, "We are here in search of a party of Santee Sioux, about ten warriors and some women. They have stolen my son's wife, who had been an Ojibwa slave of the Santee Sioux. We are here only to recover this young woman. We believe that these Santee Sioux, led by Chief Little Crow himself, are in route to Manitoba to escape the war and to join with other Sioux residing there."

In the Ojibwa tongue, Blue Feather added, "The young woman is Ojibwa, of the Fish clan; her husband, Robert, is mixed blood, part Ojibwa, of the Marten clan.

The Ojibwa leader was quiet for a few seconds as he considered this information.

"The war must be going poorly if the Santee Sioux war chief is escaping. He might be seeking to recruit Sioux warriors in Manitoba to reverse this trend. We do not want groups of Sioux traveling through our territory."

"If you join us, we can track these Santee Sioux, rescue the young woman, and make sure they return to their tribe's territory," suggested Henri.

The Ojibwa leader turned to his right-hand man who rode up beside him. The two conferred for a minute in Ojibwa, then the leader answered Henri in French, "We will help you track down these raiders and return the young woman to her husband." Turning to Blue Feather, he said in Ojibwa, "You speak our tongue well, but like someone who is not of our nation."

"You speak the truth! I am of the Osage nation, to the south in Missouri. I have tried to learn as many Indian languages as I can to be an emissary of peace among the nations."

"I see two other Indians in your posse, but they are not Ojibwa."

"John Other Day and Silver Wolf are both Santee, but they are helping the U.S. Army to put down the Sioux rebellion. Also, Robert with the dark blond hair is the son of Henri. Robert is a mixed-blood, of French, Santee, and Ojibwa ancestry."

"But what is the tribe of the small man with yellowish skin?"

"That is Yung Wing, who is from China."

"Oh, yes! I have heard of these new people!"

The new combined posse, now consisting of twenty-six men, picked up the trail of Little Crow's group and loped along at about 12 miles per hour. Their quarry (the object of their pursuit) could not be traveling faster than four miles per hour; thus, they thought they would eventually catch up and overtake them.

Just before dusk, the posse thought that they had spotted the Santee group about a mile ahead of them. The Ojibwa leader, Running Elk, conferred with Henri, "I should lead half of my braves in an arc to get in front of the Santee on their right, and my righthand man, White Elk, should lead the other half to do the same on the left. Your group should continue in this direction and approach them from the rear. We can surround them and force them to surrender."

In a matter of minutes, Little Crow and his braves found themselves confronted on the left and the right by Ojibwa bands of about ten warriors each. The Ojibwa leader put up his hand and said in passable Sioux, "Stop here and turn around! You are on Ojibwa hunting grounds. You are not welcome here!"

Hearing the man say he was Ojibwa, Linda Marie, who was not gagged, but bound hand and foot, called out in Ojibwa, "Help me! I am Linda Marie, daughter of White Dove of the Fish clan. The Santee stole me from the Ojibwa twelve years ago after they murdered my mother and father."

Two Ojibwa braves dismounted and walked up to the travois where Linda Marie was bound. Snowy Owl tried to stand in their way but was pushed aside by a tall husky brave. "I am also of the Fish clan, and we spoke of the loss of your mother and father and their little girl to the Santee. We will return you to your husband."

"No, that will be impossible. My husband is ..." And before she could complete her sentence, Robert and his posse arrived and Robert called out, "Alive and well, Linda Marie, and right behind you!"

Linda Marie screamed with joy and came running to Robert who had just dismounted. The young couple hugged each other fiercely and Linda Marie sobbed with relief. "But that fiend, Snowy Owl, showed me a scalp and said it was yours!?"

"Well, either he was lying, or he was mistaken. My friend Patrick had hair much like mine and he was killed in a cowardly sniper attack. So, it was his scalp that you saw."

"Step away from her!"

Robert and Linda Marie turned to see who was shouting that order. It was Snowy Owl, pointing a rifle at Robert.

"Snowy Owl, Linda Marie is my wife. You have no rightful claim to her! Now, look around you and count how many men have their weapons aimed at you. Put your rifle down now, and you can live."

Snowy Owl looked around him and saw that every man in Robert's group stood ready to shoot him dead. Still, he did not immediately put down his rifle. Instead, he said, "How is it that you are not dead? I shot you with my sniper rifle! Then I scalped you."

"You killed my friend, Patrick McMahon, who was also part Indian. You killed a good man, who was saving money to go to medical school and then practice medicine at an Indian reservation."

Snowy Owl lowered his rifle and walked away, averting his eyes from the stares of his tribesmen. Little Crow regarded him with disgust thinking that he had failed as a father to raise a man with honor.

Little Crow spoke up. "We will leave this place, but we want to make camp here tonight. We have some small children and some ancient ones to care for."

"You may camp here. But then leave tomorrow. My warriors will stay here until our visitors have traveled at least two hours back to their homes.

"Are you saying that you don't trust me not to pursue my enemy if you look away?" growled out Little Crow.

"Yes, that is what I am saying. And now we will stay here three hours to give these people a good head start."

"What, do you have a white man's timepiece?" sneered Little Crow.

White Elk held up his pocket watch. "Yes, I have one. Traded six beaver pelts for it!"

Little Crow just spat on the ground in disgust, "Enough of this! Women, start cooking the evening meal."

୭୭୭୭

CHAPTER TWENTY

The Journey Home and the Journey Forward

L inda Marie sat in front of Robert on his beautiful paint horse. She smiled to herself when she thought of the bravery of Robert, Henri, John, Blue Feather, and Yung Wing in coming to rescue her. But then she thought of Elfriede and had a moment of terror, "Robert, is Elfriede all right? I didn't think they took her with us, but now I am worried.

"Oh, you need not worry! Elfriede pretended to be unconscious until your abductors were out of sight. She noted their general direction and then cut through the ropes binding her on the stones of the fireplace. Then she limped back to the farm and told us what happened."

"We were blessed to have that strong brave woman on our side. Without her, I might never have been found," Linda Marie sighed and leaned back onto Robert.

"Believe me, I thank God for her," said Robert and he leaned in to kiss his bride.

Robert's group rode through the night stopping once to rest and water the horses. There was a full moon that night that lit the way more than adequately. They arrived at the Perrault farm some hours after midnight finding the yard illuminated by multiple torches and a bonfire. Sitting around the bonfire were Roseanne, Makawee, Elfriede, Josef, Karl, and Wilhelm. They jumped up when they saw the riders at the gate, and then the women greeted Linda Marie and Robert with hugs and tears of relief and joy. Makawee was so happy to see her son and his bride that she sobbed with relief. The others in the rescue party dismounted and started to take their steeds to the corral. Karl and Wilhelm took care of Brunhilde who had been taken back in tow.

"Did they hurt you?" asked Roseanne.

"They treated me roughly and lied to me, telling me that Robert was dead. All the time I was captive they had my hands and ankles bound, and for a long time, I was gagged. But Snowy Owl's mother and my mistress beat Snowy Owl with reeds before he could violate me! So, in the end, I was unharmed, at least physically. Our menfolk were courageous in pursuing Little Crow and Snowy Owl and were so smart to enlist the aid of an Ojibwa hunting party who they happened to run into while on the trail. I don't know if they helped us because they knew I was Ojibwa, but they made the right choice. There was no bloodshed, I thank God!"

"Well, it's all over now! Things will return to normal; you will have to find a way to put it out of your mind," said Roseanne.

"It will be some time before I can do that!" said Linda Marie.

"With God's help you will find peace," said Makawee.

"Ja, und we can pray for you that you find this peace soon," said Elfriede.

$$\infty\infty\infty$$

CHAPTER TWENTY-ONE

The End of the Sioux Uprising

The Santee Sioux uprising was finally put down with the victory of the U.S. Army (the Third Minnesota and the state militia) at the battle of Wood Lake, as it came to be called. Over three hundred Santee Sioux warriors were arrested and jailed at Mankato. General Sibley's superior officer, General John Pope wanted to exterminate the entire Santee Sioux tribe, but this action struck Sibley as inhumane and unwise. Instead, Sibley set up a military commission of five officers with orders to "try summarily" all Santee Sioux and mixed bloods accused of murders, robberies, or other "outrages." All accused were found guilty in a quick trial, and all were sentenced to be hanged until dead. But the President himself had to approve of this sentence; and the list of warriors who were sentenced to die was reduced to thirty-eight, with Lincoln writing out each death warrant in his own hand.

Several hundred women and girls were freed from captivity at what came to be called Camp Release. An exact count of the number of white settlers who were killed was never accomplished, but estimates have been as high as eight hundred deaths.

Some weeks after the victory over the Santee Sioux, Henri and Robert were in New Ulm buying some supplies. They were in the general store when they heard some guns firing and angry shouts from a quickly forming crowd. Robert started to run out to see what was happening, but his father grabbed his arm and pulled him back through the door.

"Robert, I don't think we should go out to the street right now. This is building up to a mad riot, and someone might be shot."

"Pa, look, the commotion is all about General Sibley and his troops marching the captured Santee warriors through the middle of town!"

The general storekeeper said with a German accent, "*Ja*, the Army is marching the *brutale Wilde* (brutal savages) to Mankato, where soon they will be swinging from ropes. I hope all of them!"

"I heard that the President himself will have to sign the death warrants," said Henri.

Another customer, an old German American farmer with a long flowing beard said, "*Das ist sicher eine übele Angelegenheit. Aber sie verdienen diese Strafe.*" The storekeeper translated for them, "This is nasty business, to be sure. But they deserve this punishment."

Henri and Robert waited in the store for the streets to calm down, then they loaded their wagon and returned home. There was plenty of rebuilding to do. Henri, John Other Day, Robert, and Silver Wolf helped the Bauer family build a new house on the original spot. The fireplace and chimney were inspected and found to be sound, so at least that part of the original house was intact. The next project was the rebuilding of the Other Days' home and his barn, both of which had been torched by the Santee. Because of the heroics of John Other Day, a large number of grateful men from New Ulm volunteered to rebuild the Other Day house and barn and both were ready for occupancy in a matter of days through the efforts of separate teams. When the same men heard of the need for a home by Robert and Linda Marie, they immediately set to work cutting timber for their house, using the forests in the Minnesota River Valley. It would take months to properly furnish these new homes and many more months before everyone felt settled again.

The public hanging of thirty-eight Santee Sioux took place at 10:00 in the morning of December 26, 1862, in Mankato. No one in either the Perrault, Bauer, or Other Day families attended. Yet, many hard feelings remained among the white settlers in Minnesota who mourned the loss of loved ones. Considerate of the sentiment among his constituents, the governor expelled all Indians from the state, removing them to a reservation in the Dakota Territory to the west. John Other Day was spared this indignity and was allowed to stay in Minnesota. Later, John was awarded a sum of $2,500 ($63,000 in 2019 dollars) which he used to buy a bigger farm near Henderson Minnesota. Then sometime later John moved to the Sisseton-Wahpeton reservation in the Dakota Territory.

Robert and Linda Marie made their home in the house built for them on the Perrault farm. Their first child, John Patrick, was born in this home in 1864. Robert continued his soldiering at Fort Ridgely and was not required to participate in the Civil War. Silver Wolf came to live with John and Roseanne until John sold his Minnesota farm and moved to the Sisseton Sioux Reservation in the Dakota Territories.

On July 5, 1863, Henri and Robert were returning from New Ulm with a wagon load of supplies when they ran into John Other Day and Blue Feather. "Did you hear the news?"

"Well at the general store in New Ulm we heard about the Union's victories at Gettysburg, Pennsylvania, and Vicksburg, Mississippi," Robert said.

"We heard that news too, but I'm speaking of something much closer to home," John replied.

Blue Feather piped in, "Yes, as it turns out Chief Little Crow didn't live much beyond the end of the Sioux Uprising. When his tribe lost their land along the Minnesota River, Little Crow and some of the Santee Sioux decided that they should return to a nomadic lifestyle. But they needed horses. So, Chief Little Crow led a raiding party from Manitoba back into Minnesota to steal some from the white farmers. Most of his people did not support his decision.

On July 3, Little Crow and his son, Wowinapa, were picking raspberries when spotted by a farmer, Natan Lamson, and his son Chauncy. There was an exchange of gunfire between the Lamsons and Little Crow and his son. Nathan Lamson was wounded, but he and his son managed to kill Little Crow. Wowinapa escaped. Once warned of an Indian raiding party, white settlers from Hutchinson rode the 12 miles to the scene of the killing. There they found the body of Little Crow wearing a coat belonging to James McGannon, who had been found dead two days earlier. The Hutchinson search party identified the dead Indian as Little Crow, and then scalped him, and dragged the corpse back to Hutchinson where they mutilated it further."

"Good grief!" said Robert. "I hope that this barbarism ends here and isn't repeated if there are future conflicts with the Indians."

"Robert, I am afraid that there will be many conflicts between white settlers and various Indian tribes when the war between the states ends, and white people push westward. I would not be surprised if white Americans deliberately set out to kill the massive herds of buffalo that the plains Indians rely on for meat and hides. Without the buffalo, their way of life will be destroyed," said Henri.

"So, we are witnessing the beginning of the end for the nomadic Indians of the plains?"

"I am afraid so." And Blue Feather and John Other Day slowly nodded in agreement. "And the innocent will suffer along with the guilty."

❧❧❧

END NOTES

[1] Four bands comprised the Santee division of the Sioux Nation, the Mdewakantonwan, Wahpeton, Sissetons, and the Wahpekute. The Santee Tribe was originally a woodlands tribe, living in semi-permanent villages and engaging in some farming.

[2] This section relies on the testimony of Chief Big Eagle as reported in *True Tales and Amazing Legends of the Old West*. New York: Clarkson Potter Publishers, 2005.

EPILOGUE

This novel is a work of historical fiction based on events leading up to and including the Sioux Rebellion of 1862. The point of the book was not to give a complete account of this war and its aftermath, but instead to give a fictional account of how some Christian families adapted to the terrifying circumstances of this conflict with the help of their faith. Some historical figures appeared as characters in the story. These included Chief Little Crow, John Other Day, Inkpaduta, Colonel Henry Hastings Sibley, and Captain John Marsh. In the case of Chief Little Crow some of his exact words were included as dialogue in this story.

Good references on the Dakota War (or Sioux Rebellion) can be found at https://www.usdakotawar.org/ and at https://en.wikipedia.org/wiki/Dakota_War_of_1862. Likewise, a good reference on Chief Little Crow appears at https://en.wikipedia.org/wiki/Little_Crow. John Other Day, a truly heroic person, is briefly discussed at https://www.usdakotawar.org/history/anpetutokeca-john-other-day. The character in this novel was developed to be consistent with this historical account.

www.ingramcontent.com/pod-product-compliance
Lightning Source LLC
Chambersburg PA
CBHW032000040426
42448CB00006B/437